PRAISE FOR **PRAYER SHIELD**

It is imperative that we learn how to pray effectively for our leaders—in churches, in organizations and in prayer movements. *Prayer Shield* is both timely and definitive. There's nothing else quite like it, designed to equip all of us to bring the covering of the Lord upon the servants of the Lord, by prayer. This is a book that must be read, now more than ever.

DAVID BRYANT
Leader, PROCLAIM HOPE!
Author *In the Gap* and *With Concerts of Prayer*

Prayer Shield is the most inspirational book I have ever read on the subject of intercession.

SUZETTE HATTINGH
Co-founder, Voice in the City

I want to give this book to every member of my church.

RICK WARREN
Senior Pastor, Saddleback Church, Lake Forest, California
Author, *The Purpose Driven Life*

D0858823

PRAYER SHIELD

HOW TO INTERCEDE FOR PASTORS AND CHRISTIAN LEADERS

C. PETER WAGNER

Bestselling Author of *Finding Your Spiritual Gifts*

Chosen

a division of Baker Publishing Group
Minneapolis, Minnesota

© 1992, 2014 by C. Peter Wagner

Published by Chosen Books
11400 Hampshire Avenue South
Bloomington, Minnesota 55438
www.chosenbooks.com

Chosen Books is a division of
Baker Publishing Group, Grand Rapids, Michigan

Chosen Books edition published 2015
ISBN 978-0-8007-9743-0

Previously published by Regal Books.

Printed in the United States of America

Library of Congress Catalog Number: 2014956821

15   16   17   18   19   20   21   7   6   5   4   3   2   1

Contents

Introduction to the Second Edition

Prayer Shield is a book very dear to my heart. Intercession for Christian leaders has grown to be one of my favorite topics. I began to understand these things and put them into practice back around 1988, and I am still very excited about them.

As this second edition goes to press, I have now reached the age where I have a good deal to look back upon. I'm not through by any means, but after logging over 60 years of ordained ministry so far, I can say that I've run a fairly good race. Hopefully I'm not arrogant or boastful by saying this; I am trying to evaluate as honestly and objectively as I can. I do not pretend to be anywhere near to being the number one Christian leader, but I think it's safe to say that I have maintained an above average standing in doing Christian ministry.

Let me put it this way: My lengthy career as a Christian leader has drawn me into some arenas of unusually high intensity, especially over the past 20 years or so. I am often asked questions like this one: "Peter, what you have been doing obviously is very upsetting to the devil. How do you cope with all the spiritual warfare that you must experience?"

My response may surprise some: "Actually, I really don't mind dealing with spiritual warfare." This statement, naturally, begs an explanation. This book gives a full explanation of why this is so, but let me give a short summary here.

I have no doubt at all that I am high on Satan's hit list of enemies who are combating his realm of darkness. I know that he would like to bring me down. I know that powerful demonic forces have been assigned to me and unleashed to terrorize me physically, materially, emotionally, socially and spiritually. Yes, I have been forced to confront some of these forces and deal with them directly from time to time. I do sense that these episodes of serious,

personal spiritual engagement have been relatively few and far between—at least in light of the rather startling testimonies of some
of my peers. I feel that I have been very fortunate, and I attribute
this good fortune to two things. First, I have been a grateful recip-
ient of God's favor and His grace. To God be all the glory! Second,
I attribute my good fortune to the influence of my personal intercessors, who open the gates of heaven so that God's grace can
continually flow into my life and my ministry. I am positive that
I would not be where I am now without them. After our immediate family, Doris and I regard our personal prayer partners as the
closest relationships we have. I think so highly of them that I have
their pictures pasted on the inside of the front cover of my Bible!

Knowing that my prayer partners are on the front lines on my
behalf, I sleep well. I go to bed around 10:30 P.M., spend a peaceful
night, and awaken around 6:30 A.M. My intercessors, on the other
hand, have told me of some of the nocturnal battles they have
fought for me. I remember one conversation that I had a few years
ago with Beth Alves, one of our personal intercessors. She greeted
me by asking how I was, and I responded that I was very well—
thanks to her. Beth got a playful look in her eyes and said, "I know
what you mean! You should see the spiritual black and blue marks
I have all over me because of you!" We both laughed, but each
of us knew that what she had just said was very true. One of her
assignments from God was to do spiritual warfare on my behalf.
Because of Beth and my other prayer partners, it is very rare that
the devil's attacks get through to me. That is why this book is titled
Prayer Shield.

During the 1970s, the Holy Spirit began to speak clearly to
many Christian leaders about the need to cover in prayer those who
were engaged in Christian ministry and related activities. This was
the beginning of one of the most far-reaching changes in modern
Christianity. Never before in living memory had prayer been such a
high agenda item for apostles, pastors, Christian leaders, ministers
in the workplace and other believers. As these leaders obeyed God's

call, the Church was brought to a new level of impact, from which we continue to benefit today.

During that first decade, I was one of the Christian leaders who, unfortunately, was unaware of what was happening. That was actually a time when I was entering the most prayerless season of my ministry. Thankfully, in the early 1980s, when I started my adult Sunday School class at Lake Avenue Church in Pasadena, California, I began to turn and experience the power of prayer. It was a slow process at first—let me explain.

In 1971 I began a 30-year tenure as Professor of Church Growth at Fuller Theological Seminary. One of my responsibilities was to analyze the factors contributing to both the growth and the decline of Christian churches worldwide. It gradually became clear that the interaction of institutional factors (which the church could control if it wished) with contextual factors (sociological conditions that churches could not control) answered most of the questions concerning church health and vitality—but not all of them. I think I might have been the first among my colleagues in the professional field of church growth to suspect that *spiritual factors* needed to be added to our list of determinants.

In 1987 I began giving major attention to prayer, even though I knew relatively little about the topic. I built a rather extensive library on prayer and read scores of volumes in order to give myself a decent grasp of the subject. My objectives were (1) to attempt to determine the areas of prayer that were adequately covered by the literature and (2) to discover any areas that were relatively underdeveloped. I felt like the Lord was assigning me to work in areas that would come to light by way of the second objective.

After months and months of study, I perceived that there were at least three obvious areas that needed to be addressed and developed: (1) strategic-level intercession or spiritual warfare dealing with principalities and powers, (2) intercession for Christian leaders, and (3) the relationship between prayer and the growth of the local church. These observations helped me establish part of my writing agenda for the 1990s. My efforts included the publication of the first edition of *Prayer Shield*, which was originally part of a six-volume series. This series covered topics such as strategic-level spiritual warfare, intercession for Christian leaders, the theory and practice of spiritual mapping, the prayer ministries of outstanding churches in America and other nations, a scholarly apologetic for strategic-level spiritual warfare, and a summary of the spiritual factors for church growth that emerged during the 1990s. I had begun to log some experience with receiving the benefits of personal intercession prior to beginning my research on prayer. I believed that the quality of my ministry moved to a higher plane as a result of receiving personal intercession. Because of this, as I read many books on prayer, I was very surprised to discover that reference to the ministry of interceding specifically for Christian leaders was minimal.

This meant that in previous generations an appallingly small amount of teaching on intercession for leaders was available. More than 100 years ago, Charles G. Finney did dedicate two pages of his classic *Lectures on Revivals of Religion* to admonishing his readers to "pray for ministers."[1] Among other things, he said, "I have known a church to bear their minister on their arms in prayer from day to day, and watch with anxiety unutterable, to see that he has the Holy Ghost with him in his labors!"[2] And later, "How different is the case, where the church feel that the *minister* is praying, and so there is no need of their praying!"[3]

As one might suspect, E. M. Bounds, arguably history's most prolific author on prayer, had something to say about praying for pastors. A chapter in his book *Power Through Prayer* (1912) is titled "Preachers Need the Prayers of the People," and a chapter in *The Weapon of Prayer* (1931) is titled "The Preacher's Cry—Pray for Us!" Bounds considered prayer for pastors so important that he stated, "Air is not more necessary to the lungs than prayer is to the preacher." He stressed, as I do in this book, "*The preacher must pray; the preacher must be prayed for*" (emphasis his).[4]

While teaching on intercession for Christian leaders may have been sparse in past generations, this is no longer the case. Many of the steady stream of books on prayer include chapters on the subject. An outstanding example is "Personal Prayer Partners," a chapter in Cindy Jacobs's classic *Possessing the Gates of the Enemy*.[5] Since *Prayer Shield* helped to break the ice, two other excellent books have appeared: *Preyed On or Prayed For* by Terry Teykl and *Partners in Prayer: Support and Strengthen Your Pastor and Church Leaders* by John Maxwell. Both of these are available from Amazon.com, and I strongly recommend them for your library.

One of the reasons I wanted to do this second edition of *Prayer Shield* is that my previous focus, and that of other authors of books on prayer, was largely on pastors. Since *Prayer Shield*'s initial publication, some seismic shifts have been moving the Church to new levels. For one thing, the New Apostolic Reformation is now being recognized as the most explosive segment of contemporary Christianity, especially in the Global South. The Second Apostolic Age began in 2001. One of the implications of this has been that Ephesians 4:11 is taken more literally than it was in the past. This is where the apostle Paul says that Jesus "gave some to be apostles, some prophets, some evangelists, and some pastors and teachers." Yes, we need to continue interceding for pastors, but we also need to include apostles, prophets, evangelists and teachers at the same level. I knew virtually nothing about apostles and apostolic ministry when the first edition of *Prayer Shield* was released, but now I have a wealth of experience—in fact, I am an apostle![6]

A second seismic shift impacting the Church has been the mushrooming agreement that the heart of the Great Commission is to make disciples of whole nations (see Matt. 28:19), leading to a commitment to the dominion mandate or the transformation of society.[7] In order to help bring this transformation about, God has allowed us to begin recognizing that the kingdom of God is not limited to the organized church as we have customarily conceived it, but that the Church functions in the workplace as well. What

God's people do in the workplace is a legitimate form of ministry. There are apostles, prophets, evangelists, pastors and teachers in the workplace, and intercession for leaders must include them as well.[8]

Once we recognized our duty to reform society, God then, through Lance Wallnau, gave us the insight we needed to understand the "Seven Mountains" that have always operated together to mold the culture in which we live. Instead of attempting to reform society in general, it becomes much more convenient and productive to attempt to reform each of the Seven Mountains simultaneously. The mountains are religion, family, education, media, government, arts and entertainment, and business.[9]

Tommi Femrite, one of our personal intercessors, was among the first to recognize that Kingdom-minded leaders in the workplace stand in just as much need of personal intercession as do traditional Church leaders, but, for certain reasons that I will discuss later, they might not be able to find intercessors who are available. Tommi has summarized her thoughts in a ground-breaking book, *Invading the Seven Mountains with Intercession*,[10] and I will refer to her work in the main part of this book.

I offer *Prayer Shield* to you to equip you to pray for Christian leaders as the Holy Spirit prompts you. Before we dive in, allow me to share the encouragement I received about *Prayer Shield* from my good friend Elmer Towns. I greatly admire Elmer for many things, not the least of which is a fact that he almost never discusses: He has authored more than 160 books! A few times, when referencing me in public, Elmer said that *Prayer Shield* was my best book. That made me curious because I have written 70 books (I am only a beginner compared to Elmer!), and I was positive that he had not read all of the other 69. However, I never thought to bring this up during our private conversations.

I was recently privileged to read Elmer's memoirs, in which he tells about reading *Prayer Shield*, which he strangely describes as "an outstanding book with a poor title."[11] At the time, the idea of personal intercessors was new to him, so he Xeroxed copies for a group of prayer warriors he had been meeting with, discussed the book with them, and gathered the courage to ask the question "Will you make my ministry your prayer ministry?"[12] The very next week, God gave him what I call an I-1 intercessor, and Elmer attributes the success he has had over the last 20 years and more primarily to the ministry of his personal prayer partners.

THE POWER OF PERSONAL PRAYER PARTNERS

When I wrote the first edition of this book, I highlighted the following statement:

> The most underutilized source of spiritual power in our churches today is intercession for Christian leaders.

Now, 20 years later, the good news is that this deficiency is gradually being corrected. I can remember the days when, if I visited a typical church and asked the pastor whether he or she had a team of personal intercessors, I would get answers like this: "My spouse is the one who prays for me. And everybody in the church knows that Sister Eleanor, who is over 70 years old and sits in the third pew every Sunday, is a wonderful prayer warrior." Or, "Everyone in the church prays for me." I soon began to recognize such responses as evasive language. These pastors did not really understand what I was talking about.

Things are a bit different now. More often than not, when I visit a new church and have time to socialize with the pastor, he or she will routinely introduce me to a church member with the rather nonchalant words, "I want you to meet so-and-so. She is one of our intercessors."

I haven't conducted scientific research in this area, but please permit me to make an educated guess. I would say that when *Prayer Shield* first came out, maybe 5 to 10 percent of Christian leaders had true personal intercessors. Today, I wouldn't be surprised if the number had risen to 50 percent or higher. I don't pretend that *Prayer Shield* was the only cause of this. In the Introduction to this edition, I tell of the remarkable quantity and quality of literature that we now have on the topic of intercession for leaders. And the phenomenon cuts across denominational lines. I'm looking forward to the day, not too long from now, when activating intercessors for leaders will be as deeply ingrained in ordinary church life as passing the offering plate!

Spiritual Brinkmanship at Skyline Wesleyan

I first connected with John Maxwell when he was senior pastor of Skyline Wesleyan Church in San Diego, California. I was Professor of Church Growth at Fuller Theological Seminary at the time, and the vigorous growth of his church had attracted my attention. During John's 14-year pastorate, Skyline grew from 1,000 to 3,300 members. Since leaving Skyline in 1995, John has become, arguably, the number one motivator and trainer of leaders in the country, with his books selling more than 20 million copies.

But back when I was first getting to know him, I quickly learned that John attributed much of the power for church growth to his team of personal intercessors. He had woven intercession for leaders into the warp and woof of his church, and he taught me much of what I know about this subject. You will see that his name comes up frequently in this book.

I offer this background to provide context for a fascinating event in which intercessory prayer narrowly averted a major mistake. It saved the church from launching out on a track that was not God's plan.

By the time Skyline had grown to almost 3,000 people, the church's old facility, located in a deteriorating section of the city, had been stretched beyond capacity. Three services on Sunday morning could not accommodate all who wanted to attend, and the growth plateaued. It became obvious to John and the other leaders that if the church was to reach all the people God had called them to reach, they would have to move to new facilities.

Finding a new site large enough to accommodate their bold, God-given vision for the future was no easy task. John knew they needed up to 100 acres in a desirable area. However, real estate agents were telling him that San Diego had experienced so much recent growth that this kind of property simply was no longer available. They should have begun looking for property 10 or 15 years previously!

By then, John had built a team of 100 men from Skyline who served as highly committed personal prayer partners. Later on I will explain how he did this, but suffice it to say at the moment that they were praying fervently with John and his leadership team as they searched for new property. John kept the intercessors thoroughly informed, but as month after month went by with no results, frustration began to mount and morale began to slip. The church remained on its growth plateau. Unfortunately, it looked like the real estate agents were right.

Then a breakthrough came! A 50-acre piece of prime real estate located right beside the freeway became available. John's team went to work, struggled through some complicated negotiations, and finally made a low offer of $2 million. Quite unexpectedly the owner accepted! The Skyline church board agreed that they had looked at all the angles, and that the decision to buy the property was correct. They chose a Sunday night for a congregational meeting to approve the board's recommendation to buy.

I don't think many pastors would have done what John then did. Even after all the fervent prayer that had already gone up concerning the new property, John characteristically wanted to make sure they had prayed enough. After all, this would be one of the most momentous decisions the church had ever made and possibly would ever make. It had to be clearly the will of God. So John said to his prayer partners, "Let's make sure, guys, that we have reached the right decision. Just in case, let's all go out to the property and pray once again!"

The results were an enormous surprise. This was the day before the crucial congregational meeting. John and his 100 prayer partners met at the site of what all believed would be the future location of Skyline. However, the more they prayed, the more they began getting a strange, rather ominous feeling—first individually, and then in groups. After some unimaginable agonizing before God, they began to admit to one another that they were hearing God say, "This is not your site!"

At the congregational meeting held the next evening, John rehearsed the process they had gone through in considering whether to purchase the property. The decision had seemed right from the business point of view, from the financial point of view, from the church management point of view, and from the advice they had received from many sources. However, one thing could trump all those positive indicators. That one thing was the word of the Lord, which had come through the earnest and effective prayer of the intercessors the night before!

Even though John knew that many frustrated and tired church members would be upset, he had enough faith in the hand of God working through his prayer partners that he became bold. He recommended that Skyline withdraw the offer for the property. Then he went on to assure the congregation that if God was really telling them not to buy this property, it was because He had something much better in store for them. No one could have imagined how prophetic that statement was to become!

The search process began once again. The team soon located a beautiful 80-acre property and asked the owners twice if they would sell. They were turned down both times, but the prayer partners continued to pray. Soon a serious financial issue arose, causing the owners to be more disposed to get rid of the land. John made an opening offer of $1.8 million for the 80 acres. By then the owners had found themselves in such a tight situation that they reluctantly agreed to sell—but only under certain conditions. If for any reason Skyline could not get the land zoned for a church, they would return the land and pay the owners interest on what the church had spent.

As they moved forward, the church found that somehow they were forced to buy three times the usual number of shares of water rights in order to get permission for development. That meant they had to pay $120,000 for the water rights. But just then a serious drought set in on southern California. Because of the drought, the former owners asked the church to sell two-thirds of the water rights back to them. The church used that leverage to persuade the owners to drop the agreement that the church would have to give back the property if it was not zoned for a church. So the church got the 80 acres for $1.8 million with no restrictions—and by then the value of two-thirds of the water rights had soared to $250,000, giving the church a profit of $130,000 on that part of the transaction!

It gets better! Skyline had their new 80 acres surveyed and discovered that their land was actually 110 acres. Then the Water District said that they needed 10 acres from the lower part of the property and in exchange they offered to trade 30 acres at the top, right where John had envisioned the parking lot. That meant that instead of the original 80 acres, the church then had 130 acres!

Finally, as frosting on the cake, another company offered $4 million for a stretch of industrial-zoned land that the church did not need anyway. This paid off the original $1.8 million with a surplus for the church of $2.2 million. Skyline ended up with an ideal church site plus money to spare! Since then, not only did they build on that property, but they also eventually outgrew it, and the senior pastor at this writing, Jim Garlow, has moved the congregation into a newer, larger and more modern facility.

Why did I decide to tell this rather long but quite exciting story? Because this is a chapter on the power of prayer partners. Think about it. John Maxwell's prayer partners went to pray over a piece of land that was supposed to be a done deal—but they clearly heard the Lord say, "No!" John then had the courage to take that unpopular word to the congregational meeting, and the offer to buy the property was withdrawn. Once that was done, doors began to open miraculously, and Skyline was able to move strongly into its next season!

Keep in mind that Skyline Wesleyan Church does not have an exclusive franchise on this kind of prayer power. God wants to release similar power in your church as well, and this book will help you tune in to the ways and means of seeing that done. The best days for you, your pastor, your apostolic leadership, and your ministers in the workplace might also be just ahead!

God's Pattern of Power

Is what I have just said biblical? As we move on we will see that the Bible strongly supports the principle of spiritual power being released through personal intercessors. For a starter, let's consider the story of Moses and Joshua told in Exodus 17.

You may recall that the Amalekites had risen up as enemies of Israel. When the time came for a war, Moses called upon Joshua, his designated successor, to lead the Israelite army into battle. The two armies clashed in a valley called Rephidim, where they fought all day. The outcome? "Joshua defeated Amalek and his people with the edge of the sword" (Exod. 17:13). Simply put, Joshua went down in military history as the general who won the battle of Rephidim.

But there is much more to the story.

When Moses sent Joshua out to battle, he told him that he (Moses) would go to the top of a nearby hill and intercede for him (Joshua). On the hill overlooking the battle, Moses soon observed that while his hands were lifted up, Joshua was winning. However, when his hands were down, Joshua was losing. Moses quickly caught on and decided that he needed to do whatever it would take to keep his hands up. Aaron and Hur, who were accompanying Moses, had him sit on a stone, and for the rest of the day they were able to keep Moses' hands, holding his rod of authority, in the air. The result? Joshua prevailed and won the battle.

This is a simple story, but it has an awesome principle for us to keep in mind. Joshua is fighting while Moses is praying. Joshua gets credit for winning the battle, but we know who really won it. Ultimately, of course, it was God's power that provided the victory. However, the human agent most directly used as a vehicle for that divine power to be released was the intercessor, Moses, not the general, Joshua. I would dare to speculate that, if Moses hadn't been interceding, Joshua would have lost the battle!

One of Walter Wink's best-known quotations is "History belongs to the intercessors."[1] Here is a perfect biblical example of how God used an intercessor to determine the course of history.

Think of Joshua for a moment. We could say that Joshua was the one "doing the ministry." It so happened that his God-given "ministry" assignment on that particular day was to fight a battle. Now, how much do you think Joshua was actually praying during the battle? Probably very little, if at all. Yet the battle was ultimately won by prayer—not the prayers of the "minister," but the prayers of the intercessor. I do not mean to imply that Joshua was unimportant. The battle could not have been won without him either.

Many Christian leaders today are like Joshua. They are active in ministry, some in the church and some in the workplace. They are winners. People regard them as powerful servants of God. Day after day the power of God flows through them for the benefit of others. What releases this power? In many cases it is released through intercession.

Somebody "Prayed the Price!"

A great example of this principle comes from my friend Larry Lea. Larry had just finished seminary and was serving as youth minister at Beverly Hills Baptist Church in Dallas. The church was growing well, and so was Larry's youth group. He had 1,000 teenagers in his group; it was one of the largest youth groups in the area. Then Larry received his first invitation to preach a citywide evangelistic crusade. The city was Hereford, Texas—population 15,853. Larry had felt that one of his stronger gifts was that of an evangelist, and he had great faith that God would give him a significant harvest of souls in Hereford.

The format was that Larry would preach each night in a different one of the cooperating churches. The first night, he preached his heart out and gave the invitation—but nobody came. He was very disappointed. The second night, the same thing happened. This was totally unexpected! Larry began trying to figure out what could be going wrong. The sermons were well structured. They were theologically sound. The gospel was clear. Larry's biggest worry? *What will I say when I get back to Dallas and report to my youth group?*

The third night, the meeting was held in the Methodist church. Larry had arrived a bit early; two women approached him. They saw that he was nervous, so after they introduced themselves, they said, "Don't worry, Brother Lea. We've prayed for you today for eight hours!" They asked if they could lay hands on him and pray for him there. After they had prayed, one of the women said to him, "Does the phrase, 'It is finished,' mean anything to you?" Yes it did! It was the text for Larry's sermon that night. When he gave the invitation, 100 people came forward to get saved!

The next night, Larry looked for the two women and soon found them. They prayed for him again. Then the other woman asked him if he remembered the woman with the issue of blood. Yes, he did! Again, it was the text he had chosen for that evening!

By the time the week was over, 500 people had responded to the preaching and had made decisions for Christ. Larry was elated. On the flight back to Dallas, he began rehearsing to himself how he would share the good news of his successful crusade with his youth group. Then, in a quiet moment, Larry clearly heard the voice of God coming to him and saying, "Son, you had nothing to do with that revival. The reason those people got saved was that somebody *prayed the price!*"

It was then and there that Larry Lea learned the value of personal intercession for leaders. He was the Joshua on the battlefield—in this case, the evangelist who went down in history as leading 500 people to Christ in Hereford, Texas. But the truth is that the power of God to do this was released by two women who, like Moses, faithfully did the work of intercession.[2]

What Is Intercession?

We often use the word "intercession" as a synonym for "prayer." In ordinary conversation it is probably acceptable to use the words interchangeably, but not when we are dealing with them as technical terms. Prayer, generally speaking, simply means talking with God. Intercession is coming to God on behalf of another. Coming to God can involve not only words, but also actions. A good example would be Moses lifting up the serpent so that God would heal people from snake bites.

"Intercession" is derived from the Latin *inter*, meaning "between," and *cedere,* meaning "to go." Intercession, then, is going between—or, to use a biblical expression, "standing in the gap." Through Ezekiel the prophet, the Lord says, "I sought for a man among them who would make a wall, and *stand in the gap* before Me on behalf of the land, that I should not destroy it; but I found no one" (Ezek. 22:30, emphasis added). This is a clear reference to intercession, or, sadly, the lack of it.

To put it theologically: "Intercession is the act of pleading by one who in God's sight has a right to do so in order to obtain mercy for one in need."[3] Do not miss the point that a legitimate intercessor must be one who has God's endorsement and approval. Unfortunately, some intercession falls short because the intercessor does not have the proper standing before God.

Esther Stands in the Gap

The book of Esther provides us with a powerful biblical analogy of the function of an intercessor.

Esther's story has been told frequently. A mighty king of Persia, who lived more than 400 years before Christ, was named Ahasuerus in Hebrew and Xerxes in Greek. He ruled the whole Middle East from India to Ethiopia. Ahasuerus fell in love with a beautiful Jewish woman, Esther, and made her his queen without even knowing (or caring) that she was a Jew.

Then Haman, whom Ahasuerus had appointed captain of the princes, appeared on the scene. He was so egotistical that he required everyone who came into contact with him to bow down. However, Esther's uncle, Mordecai, refused to bow down to any human being, including Haman, and that got him into trouble. Once Haman learned that his new enemy, Mordecai, was a Jew, he vengefully plotted a holocaust "to destroy, to kill, and to annihilate all the Jews" in all of Persia (Esther 3:13). Mordecai got wind of the plot and asked Esther to stand in the gap with Ahasuerus on behalf of her people.

The royal custom in those days prohibited anyone, even a queen, from initiating an audience with the king. One could speak to the king only if first spoken to. Violation of this protocol incurred the death penalty. Esther knew this, but still she risked her life, approached the king, and told him of Haman's wicked intentions. The king responded favorably, executed Haman, and then worked around the tricky laws of the Medes and Persians so that the Jewish people could be saved.

How is this an analogy for the ministry of intercession?

First, Ahasuerus, politically speaking, was omnipotent within his kingdom. In that respect, he would represent God. Haman, then, would represent Satan—who comes to steal, to kill, and to destroy (see John 10:10). Esther is the intercessor who goes to God in order to neutralize the plans of Satan. How did she know that she was supposed to do that? We could say that Mordecai would represent the Holy Spirit in communicating the will of God in this matter to Esther.

In the course of this book, I will name and describe many contemporary intercessors. They bear an astounding resemblance to Esther. Esther was humble, not arrogant, even though she was a queen. She was submissive to authority. She was tuned in to the voice of God and willing to obey what she heard, even at the risk of her life. She was dependent on what we would now refer to as the Body of Christ, asking her fellow Jews to support her in prayer and fasting. She herself fasted for three days. When she felt that she was in tune with God spiritually, she was willing to say, "I will go to the king, which is against the law; and if I perish, I perish!" (Esther 4:16).

When Esther courageously approached the throne of the king, she was not placed under arrest—she was welcomed! Why? Because of a previously developed love relationship. She loved the king and he loved her. As Alice Smith would say, Esther had previously gone "beyond the veil."[4] This tells us that maintaining a special intimacy with God is a high priority for intercessors. Because Esther stood in the gap, the king used his power to save the people of God. As today's intercessors freely testify, the highest reward of the ministry of intercession is to be received in love by the Father and to see His power released for good through their intercession.

The Amazing Power of Intercession

Some may be asking at this point, "Do you really mean that the petition of a mere human being can influence the actions of an almighty and all-powerful God?" Think about the implications of that question for a moment or two. Doesn't God have everything that is ever going to happen predetermined, so that nothing we humans might do could possibly change it? This is no small matter. It is a key question for our Christian faith. Let's put it another way: Does what we do really matter for God?

I'm sure that this question has come up in your mind from time to time. Well, the answer is yes. Yes, you can be assured that what you do really matters! This is the way the almighty God chose to design the world and to structure His relationship with His people. How about Esther? I think it is safe to conclude that if Esther (or someone else God would have raised up if she had said no to His call) had not stood in the gap, the Jews would have been annihilated. Worldwide, today's Jews still honor Esther's courageous intercession as they celebrate their survival in the annual Feast of Purim.

Similarly, today's intercessors are sure that in many cases, without their faithful ministry of intercession, God would not have done the things He did. Do you think that Joshua would have won the battle of Rephidim without the intercession of Moses?

I like the way Dutch Sheets puts this. He reminds us that God asks us to pray that His kingdom will come. But isn't this already His will? We're supposed to ask for our daily bread. But doesn't He know our needs before we ask? Yes, these things are God's will. "Why then," inquires Sheets, "am I supposed to ask Him for something He already wants to do if it's not that my asking somehow releases Him to do it?"[5]

John Wesley is frequently quoted as saying, "God will do nothing on earth except in answer to believing prayer."[6] John Calvin, in his *Institutes*, affirmed that "words fail to explain how necessary prayer is."[7] Calvin believed that the providence of God does not exclude the exercise of human faith. While the Keeper of Israel neither slumbers nor sleeps, he wrote, "Yet. . . he is inactive, as if forgetting us, when he sees us idle and mute."[8]

Today's leaders, from Jack Hayford to Walter Wink, are saying the same thing. Hayford writes, "You and I can help decide which of these two things—blessing or cursing—happen on earth. We will determine whether God's goodness is released toward specific situations or whether the power of sin and Satan is permitted to prevail. Prayer is the determining factor."[9]

Walter Wink also rejects the idea that God Himself is the only cause of all that happens here on earth. God is omnipotent, but He has limited His actions on earth, in part out of respect for the freedom of His creatures. While affirming that prayer changes us, Wink adds, "It also changes what is possible for God."[10]

I would like to summarize this section on the power of intercession with a profound statement from Dutch Sheets. You will probably need to read it slowly and more than once to absorb the revelation that Sheets is bringing: "Does the fact that He is sovereign mean He operates independently of us humans, always accomplishing His will, regardless of our actions? 'NO!' As incredible as it sounds, *a sovereign God made a sovereign choice to limit Himself in many ways and situations to the actions, decisions, and requests of human beings*" (caps and italics his).[11] I could not agree more.[12]

God's Best: Moses and Samuel

If I am not mistaken, the two greatest intercessors in the Old Testament were Moses and Samuel. How would I know? God says in Jeremiah 15:1, "Even if Moses and Samuel stood before Me, My mind would not be favorable toward this people." As Dutch Sheets just said, God has chosen to allow many things that He does to depend on certain human actions and intercession; however, He has chosen to do some things no matter what. Intercessors are not manipulators of God. This is a case where God has decided what He is going to do; to reinforce His point, He makes mention of what could well be His two best intercessors, Moses and Samuel, who even together could not change His mind.

I have already mentioned Moses' intercession for Joshua during the battle of Rephidim (see Exod. 17). Another, even more dramatic, example came when Moses went up to Mount Sinai to receive the tablets of the law, and while he was gone, the people of Israel decided to turn against God and revert to paganism. God was so angry that He said, "Let Me alone, that My wrath may burn hot against them and I may consume them" (Exod. 32:10). Moses then prayed one of the most touching prayers of intercession recorded in Scripture. The result? "The Lord relented from the harm which He said He would do to His people" (Exod. 32:14).

Moses' heart was typical of many intercessors I know. He had such burning compassion for those for whom he was interceding that he said to God, "Yet now, if You will forgive their sin—but if not, I pray, blot me out of Your book which You have written" (Exod. 32:32). No wonder God regarded Moses as one of the best!

And Samuel? An outstanding example of Samuel's intercession came when the Philistines were descending on Israel. Israel was terrified; they knew they were outnumbered. So what did they do? They wisely went to the proven intercessor, Samuel, and said, "Do not cease to cry out to the Lord our God for us, that He may save us from the hand of the Philistines" (1 Sam. 7:8). In response to this plea, the intercessor sprang into action: "Then Samuel cried out to the Lord for Israel, and the Lord answered him" (1 Sam. 7:9). The Lord sent thunder upon the Philistines, they became confused, and Israel overcame them.

Samuel showed his intercessor's heart when he later said, "Far be it from me that I should sin against the Lord in ceasing to pray for you" (1 Sam. 12:23). We can be thankful that this type of intercession is not simply a part of ancient history, but that today God has given us many, many of His children with hearts like Samuel and Moses. They are precious gifts to the Body of Christ.

Intercession Resources

This is not a book on intercession in general, but rather on personal intercession for Christian leaders. The Church today is blessed with an enormous and still growing selection of up-to-date resources on prayer and intercession, some of them dating from the 1980s, but most from the 1990s onward. Please try to obtain and read *Intercessory Prayer* by Dutch Sheets; *The Power of*

Persistent Prayer by Cindy Jacobs; *Intercessors* by Elizabeth (Beth) Alves, Barbara (Tommi) Femrite and Karen Kaufman; *Praying with Authority* by Barbara Wentroble; *The Advocates* by Eddie and Alice Smith; *Prayer Storm* by James Goll; and my book, *Praying with Power.* Reading these books would be like taking a college course on the subject. You will be very well informed as well as highly motivated!

Personal Intercession in the New Testament: The Apostles

Now let's focus on personal intercession. In order to do that, I want to consider two of the most prominent apostles of New Testament times, namely Peter and Paul. Not only do we have a good deal of information concerning these two apostles and intercession, but we also even have the names of some of their chief intercessors. Let's look at them one at a time.

The Apostle Peter

One day Peter found himself in deep trouble. King Herod had awakened that morning and decided to gain favor with the Jews in Palestine by putting two Christian apostles, James and Peter, on his hit list. He summarily executed James (see Acts 12:1-2). Then he arrested Peter, imprisoned him in maximum security, chained him to two soldiers, and planned to kill him right after the Passover holidays were finished. But, try as he would, he couldn't execute Peter like he had James. Peter experienced a miraculous escape from prison because something was going on that we do not hear about with James, namely that "constant prayer was offered to God for him by the church" (Acts 12:5). Some people connected with Peter apparently understood the power of personal intercession!

Who were these people? Here is where we learn of the person who undoubtedly served as Peter's chief intercessor (whom I will later classify as an I-1 intercessor). The first place Peter went after he escaped from jail was to the house in which the believers had been praying for him—the house belonging to Mary, the mother of John Mark. It doesn't take much stretch of the imagination to surmise that Mary was Peter's I-1 intercessor. She had done what any responsible personal intercessor would have done in the midst of such happenings. She immediately got in touch with as many other intercessors as she could, and invited them to her home for a lengthy prayer vigil. How powerful was their prayer? Peter's life was spared, and Herod ended up being eaten by worms (see Acts 12:23)!

The Apostle Paul

The apostle Paul knew a great deal about personal intercession. He constantly gave receiving intercession a high priority. Through his epistles, we know that he specifically requested personal intercession at least five times.[13] He asked the Thessalonians to "pray for us" (1 Thess. 5:25). Some scholars say that the "us" is an editorial plural, and that Paul was really requesting intercession for himself. Here's what Paul said to the Romans: "Now I beg you, brethren, through the Lord Jesus Christ, and through the love of the Spirit, that you strive together with me in prayers to God for me" (Rom. 15:30). He went on to ask them to pray specifically for his coming trip to Jerusalem and for protection from his enemies (see v. 31).

In his second letter to the Corinthians, Paul tells of his narrow escape from death in Asia, and commends the Corinthians for "helping together in prayer for us, that thanks may be given by many persons on our behalf for the gift granted to us through many" (2 Cor. 1:11). Reading between the lines, this could mean that Paul felt he was delivered from death by intercession, just as we saw that Peter was. Paul writes to the Philippians from his prison cell in Rome, saying, "For I know that this will turn out for my deliverance through your prayer and the supply of the Spirit of Jesus Christ" (Phil. 1:19). Also from prison, he writes directly to Philemon: "I trust that through your prayers I shall be granted to you" (Philem. 1:22).

Remember the two women, Euodia and Syntyche, referred to in Paul's letter to the Philippians (see Phil. 4:2-3)? I believe that they were Paul's personal prayer partners. Not many commentators on Philippians recognize this, so I will try to give a good explanation. Ralph Martin's comment is typical: "Possibly [Euodia and Syntyche] assisted [Paul] with material help as Lydia had done some years before."[14] Many assume that these two women accompanied Paul to cook his meals, wash his clothes, and perform other traditionally feminine tasks.

There are, however, a few commentators who do see Euodia and Syntyche as playing a much more crucial spiritual role in Paul's ministry. F. F. Bruce, for example, points out that the Greek verb behind "labored with me in the gospel" (v. 3) is a very strong verb. He says, "Whatever form these two women's collaboration with Paul in his gospel ministry may have taken, it was not confined to making tea for him and his circle—or whatever the first-century counterpart to that activity was."[15]

The verb to which Bruce refers is the Greek *synathleo*, which means that they "contended" or "strived" or "fought at my side." Edmond Hiebert says the term "implies united action in the face of opposition and strife," so Paul's metaphor "pictures these women as having served Paul's fellow soldiers in the battle to establish the gospel in Philippi."[16] This is the language of intercession as spiritual warfare, which is exactly the way that F. W. Beare sees it. He argues that these two courageous women were "pitted along with Paul 'against principalities and powers . . . against the spiritual hosts of wickedness in the heavenly places' of Ephesians 6:12."[17]

I have taken the pains to quote these recognized scholars in order to give some academic credibility to my own personal conclusion. I believe that when Paul says that Euodia and Syntyche "labored with me in the gospel," a much more explicit translation would be, *"They did spiritual warfare on my behalf."* This is an accurate description of what my own personal intercessors have been doing for years. Let me conclude this chapter with a story involving two of Doris's and my personal intercessors; this incident shows that much intercession is, indeed, spiritual warfare.

Intercession Is Spiritual Warfare

Jane Pratt of Dallas has been one of our personal intercessors for many years. At one time, she was linked to the Eastern European Seminary and had been called as a personal intercessor for John Maisel, the president of the seminary's mission organization.

In the days shortly after the Iron Curtain had come down, John was making another of his frequent trips to the Eastern bloc. Among the highlights of his ministry were presenting a lecture on "Is Jesus God?" at Moscow State University and later preaching the gospel to a crowd of more than 20,000 in Bucharest. While John was in Europe, Jane was in Dallas doing spiritual warfare on his behalf. The lecture had a profound impact on many who heard it. A great number of souls were saved in Bucharest. You can imagine that the forces of darkness were greatly upset not only by John's ministry, but also by the divine power that flowed through Jane's intercession.

What happened then shows clearly how intercession for Christian leaders is, in essence, spiritual warfare.

On one of the nights when John was in Europe, Jane was awakened at 2:00 A.M. by the tangible presence of an incredible force of darkness there in her bedroom. She says, "I battled in prayer and still it was more than I could handle. It drained my whole energy and life support system. I couldn't move—I was totally paralyzed!" As Jane communed with the Holy Spirit, she was assured that John himself was in no particular danger at that time. She sensed that "this powerful force of darkness had been sent to destroy John, but it had attacked me because I was standing in the gap." As the battle was reaching its peak, Jane desperately cried out for reinforcements, both intercessors and angels. God heard her prayer and sent both!

In the twinkling of an eye, Jane sensed a powerful angel come into the room and usher out the spirit of darkness. The battle was over, but Jane felt limp and drained. Then both a fever and laryngitis set in. But still she rejoiced that the victory had been the Lord's!

The next morning, Jane discovered that the answering machine in her office had recorded a message from Cindy Jacobs. Cindy is another of Doris's and my 19 close personal prayer partners. Jane returned the call and routinely asked Cindy how she felt. Cindy's response was unforgettable. "I'm fine, Jane," she replied, "but the question is how are *you*? What was that incredible force of darkness in your room at two o'clock this morning? That was one of the most powerful principalities I have encountered! I was doing battle with you in intercession until its power was finally broken!"

Both Jane and Cindy are veteran spiritual warriors. Although the intensity of this battle was unusual, incidents similar to this are not. As intercessors, they expect frequent bouts with the spirits of wickedness that are out to destroy the work of God. I agree with Edwin Stube, who says, "Intercessory prayer is warfare, and the principal way in which the warfare is carried on. The warfare has to be won first in prayer and then worked out in practice."[18]

Reflection Questions

1. Talk about the theory that prayer prevented John Maxwell and Skyline Wesleyan from purchasing the wrong property. Could anyone prove this in a court of law?
2. Review the biblical meaning of "intercession." From your own experience, try to give examples of how intercession has made a difference.
3. The incident of Cindy Jacobs knowing what was happening to Jane Pratt is unusual. Have you ever experienced anything like this?

4. List two or three examples you know about of someone praying for another person and having their prayers answered.

5. What did Paul mean when he affirmed that his prayer partners were doing spiritual warfare on his behalf?

THE INTERCESSORS

Have you ever heard of the "Pareto Principle"?

A famous Italian scientist named Vilfredo Pareto made an amazing discovery a couple of hundred years ago. He found that, no matter what system of taxation was used by a given country, around 20 percent of the people controlled 80 percent of the money. Since then, the Pareto Principle has been applied to a wide variety of contexts. Just as a sample:

- 20 percent of insurance salespeople sell 80 percent of the insurance.
- 20 percent of a book will give you 80 percent of its relevant content.
- 20 percent of fishers catch 80 percent of the fish.
- 20 percent of church members give 80 percent of the budget.

And so on. You can play with this yourself, and most of the time you'll be right. The 20-80 ratio is not necessarily an exact proportion, but it does suggest an important underlying principle: *"The law of the vital few and the trivial many."*

Intercessors: "The Vital Few"

As I have studied intercession and intercessors over the course of many years, I have found that the Pareto Principle generally applies. However, the ratio does not come out to 20 percent of church members doing 80 percent of the meaningful intercession. Are you ready for a surprise? The best I can calculate, about 5 percent of the members of the average congregation provide 80 percent of the meaningful intercession. Those 5 percent would constitute the "vital few" of the Pareto formula.

I am fully aware that what I have just said will seem odd to many. If that includes you, please bear with me. Some will argue that every good church member should be interceding at a high level, not just 5 percent of them. Others will say that it is an insult to imply that the 95 percent of the members who may not pray at the level of the others should be regarded as "the trivial many." No believer is "trivial." I understand comments like these, and I sympathize with them—at least to a point. Frequently, however, reality turns out to differ from our deepest wishes.

When all is said and done, in most cases the Pareto Principle will apply. (If you sit back and take a fresh look at your congregation, you will likely see a similar proportion to what I have observed in many churches.) Yes, there are exceptions, but the exceptions tend to prove the rule. Even though every believer is expected to pray, only a relatively small number of parishioners are recognized by themselves as well as by others in the congregation as outstanding pray-ers.

Waymon Rodgers, who pastored a large church in Kentucky, often told the story of a man in his church who came up to him and said, "I want the keys to the church. I would like to pray in the church." When Rodgers told the man that the church was open every day at 8:00 A.M., he responded, "You don't understand. I used to get up and go to work at 4:30 A.M., but I'm now retired, and I want to give that time to prayer and fasting." As you would imagine, he was given his set of keys to the church, and he faithfully prayed there from 4:00 to 7:00 every morning. The other church members didn't get sets of keys.

Any pastor knows what a mistake it would be to try to lay a guilt trip on the whole congregation by saying, "If this brother can do it, anyone can do it. From now on I want all of us praying here at the church at 4:00 A.M." It would be totally unrealistic. Instead, the man should be welcomed and encouraged as one of the vital few when it comes to the prayer ministry of the church.

Just who are these vital few? They are the ones to whom God has given the *spiritual* gift of intercession.

Spiritual Gifts

In order to understand the gift of intercession as thoroughly as possible, we must first come to terms with the basic biblical teaching on spiritual gifts in general. The apostle Paul said, "Now concerning spiritual gifts, brethren, I do not want you to be ignorant" (1 Cor. 12:1).

The Body of Christ functions in many respects like a human body. Paul wrote, "As we have many members in one body [this refers to the human body], but all the members do not have the same function, so we, being many, are one body in Christ" (Rom. 12:4-5). I believe that this analogy gives us an important clue for understanding what spiritual gifts are and how they operate.

If it is true that we are all members of the Body, how, then, can we know which member we might be? How do we know if we happen to be a nose or a toe or a kidney or an eyelid? We know by discovering what spiritual gift or gifts we have. "As each one has received a gift, minister it to one another, as good stewards of the manifold grace of God" (1 Pet. 4:10).

God has given one or more spiritual gifts to every believer. No one is left out. It is interesting to note that some of our public school districts offer special programs for so-called gifted children. This would not work in our churches because all, not just some, are gifted. Not that we all have the same gifts. Some are ears and some are eyes, but the ear must not say, "Because I am not an eye, I am not of the body" (1 Cor. 12:16). The better we know our gifts, the better we can serve God in the church and in the workplace.

The Body of Christ, both in the institutional church and in the workplace, is so complex that God wisely does not leave it up to us to choose our own gifts. If He did, too many would probably decide to be eyes. After all, who would choose to be a liver instead of an eye? If you think about it, though, the human body can live without an eye, but not without a liver. That's why the Bible says, "Those members of the body which seem to be weaker are necessary" (1 Cor. 12:22). No matter what gift each of us has, we all need one another.

God Chooses Our Gifts

Only God knows each of us well enough to decide what part of the Body we should be. The Holy Spirit distributes gifts "to each one individually as He wills" (1 Cor. 12:11). God has set the members of the Body "just as He pleased" (1 Cor. 12:18). The gifts we receive come strictly at God's discretion and by His grace. The biblical word most often used for spiritual gift, charisma, contains the Greek word for grace, *charis*. This means that we do not work for our gifts and receive them as rewards. No. God graciously and wisely bestows them on us.

What, then, is our individual responsibility? As believers, one of our highest priorities in living the Christian life should be to discover what gifts God has chosen to give us. Once we know what they are, we are to be "good stewards" of them. That stewardship involves developing the gifts that we have and then using them in ministry for the glory of God.

How Many Gifts Are There?

A textbook on anatomy would tell us how many different parts the human body has. Fortunately, the Body of Christ is not that complex. Opinions differ as to exactly how many spiritual gifts there are. The research that I have done and summarized in my textbook, *Your Spiritual Gifts Can Help Your Church Grow*, leads me to suggest that there are 28, although I respect the conclusions of others who arrive at different numbers.

How do I arrive at 28 gifts?

First, I recognize three major lists of spiritual gifts in the New Testament, namely Romans 12, 1 Corinthians 12 and Ephesians 4. None of the three lists is complete in itself—there is significant overlap. Some gifts are mentioned in one list only, some in two, and some in all three. A composite of the three lists gives us 20 gifts: prophecy, service, teaching, exhortation, giving, leadership, mercy, wisdom, knowledge, faith, healings, miracles, discerning of spirits, tongues, interpretation of tongues, apostle, helps, administration, evangelist and pastor.

Five additional spiritual gifts are mentioned in the New Testament apart from the three major lists. They include: celibacy (1 Cor. 7:7), voluntary poverty (1 Cor. 13:3), hospitality (1 Pet. 4:9-10), martyrdom (1 Cor. 13:3), and missionary (Eph. 3:6-9). This gives us a total of 25 spiritual gifts listed as such in the New Testament.

Did you notice that the gift of intercession is not one of them? That's why this next principle is very important. Think about these questions: If none of the three major lists of spiritual gifts is complete in itself, and if the composite of the three is not complete either, could it be that the total of 25 gifts mentioned as such in the New Testament is also an open-ended list? If so, might there be some spiritual gifts operative in the Body of Christ that are not directly labeled as gifts in the New Testament? You probably will have guessed that I think the answer to both of these questions is yes. In fact, I would add three, completing my list of 28 gifts.

If you research this, you will find a number of other scholars and authors who agree that there are more than 25 gifts. Three additional gifts that frequently come up are craftsmanship, preaching and writing, but I have chosen not to include those in my list. The three that I do add are deliverance, leading worship, and intercession. For one thing, all three are biblical *ministries* even though they might not be labeled explicitly as *gifts*, and for another, I believe I have seen each one of them fully operative in practice.

Please let me brief you on what I think about deliverance and leading worship before I move into the rest of the chapter on the spiritual gift of intercession.

The Gift of Deliverance

The activity of demons is increasingly being recognized as a spiritual problem in churches across the theological spectrum. In response, many churches have launched deliverance ministries. I believe that every Christian has been given the authority to cast out demons in the name of Jesus. However, even in churches that have preached and practiced deliverance for some time, certain individuals seem to rise above the rest in their ability to confront and to expel evil spirits. Who are these people? For the most part, they are those to whom God has decided to give the spiritual gift of deliverance.

My wife, Doris, has this gift of deliverance. I clearly recall one Sunday morning when we were members of Lake Avenue Church in Pasadena, California. Pastor Paul Cedar preached a sermon on divine healing. That in itself was quite unexpected. But afterward, instead of inviting those who needed healing to go to the nearby prayer room, as he routinely did, he asked those who needed physical healing to come forward. So many responded that the church prayer team was overwhelmed! Pastor Cedar then invited those in the congregation who knew how to pray for the sick to come and help. Just to make sure, he said, "Will Peter and Doris Wagner please come forward?"

I prayed for one woman who had scoliosis—quite a noticeable curvature of the spine. The presence of God was strong in the sanctuary, and He moved so powerfully in this woman's back that I could feel the vertebrae moving and crunching under my hand as her spine straightened up! As I was finishing, I noticed out of the corner of my eye that my friend Phyllis Bennett was patiently waiting for me.

I had known Phyllis and her husband, David, for some time. David had been a pastor on our church staff, and then he had pastored some other churches in the area. He actually performed the wedding of our oldest daughter, Karen. At the time of this incident, he happened to be working on a doctorate at the Fuller School of World Mission (now School of Intercultural Studies), where I was teaching. The Bennetts had recently spent a few months in India, where David was doing some field research.

Phyllis told me that she had been suffering from a terrible pain in her chest, which her doctor had been unable to diagnose. Since her condition included symptoms similar to those caused by an ulcer, her doctor had put her on ulcer medication, even though an ulcer had not shown up on the X-ray (20 percent of ulcers go undiagnosed from X-rays). Her pain, however, was not responding to the medical treatment she was receiving. Then she showed me an ugly rash on her left forearm where the flesh had actually begun to fall off in chunks!

As I prayed for Phyllis's healing, I sensed, as is true from time to time (at least for me), that nothing at all was happening—just the opposite of what I had experienced with the previous woman I had prayed for. When I finished, I began offering Phyllis some nice words of consolation and faith, knowing full well that the ulcer—or whatever it was—was still there. Unbeknownst to me, however, Doris had just finished praying for another person and had quietly come up beside me.

No sooner had we made eye contact than an intense look came over Doris's face. She gently but firmly pushed me to one side, and then she took over! The Spirit of God was prompting her to take a different approach. She told Phyllis to look into her eyes, and almost instantly she locked horns in the unseen world with a demonic spirit that she knew Phyllis had picked up through a curse while she was in India!

Casting out demons was not the usual Sunday fare in our Congregational Church sanctuary on Sunday mornings, but Doris was experienced enough to bind the demon and not allow it to speak or manifest in any way. After a minute or two, Phyllis's eyes opened wide with a look of terror—as if she were watching a horror movie—and her body briefly jerked around! Then total peace. The evil spirit was gone!

The pain in Phyllis's chest was instantly healed! It left immediately. She went back to her doctor, who took her off the medication. Two weeks later, she passed me in her car, rolled down the window, and held out her left arm. The rash was well on its way to disappearing. It had been caused by the medication she had been taking for the "ulcer."

Now here is the point: I have a spiritual gift of healing, and I see quite a few people healed when I pray for them. However, if it had not been for Doris and her spiritual gift of deliverance, Phyllis would likely still have had her "ulcer." I myself had no sense at all that we were dealing with anything more than a physical malady. But this is how the Body of Christ is supposed to work. "The eye cannot say to the hand, 'I have no need of you'" (1 Cor. 12:21).

Experiences like this encourage me to believe that we do well to add the gift of deliverance to our list of spiritual gifts.

Leading Worship

I will not go into as much detail here, but I also believe that we should add the spiritual gift of leading worship to our list of gifts. Those who have the gift of leading worship are more than good musicians. True, musical ability is part of the mix, but it does not necessarily follow that the better the musician, the better the worship leader. That's why I cannot agree with some who refer to the "gift of music." I think the "gift of leading worship" is a more accurate way to describe this gift.

Along those lines, here is what recognized worship leader Ron Kenoly says: "[God] wants us to create a place where He can come and receive from us whatever's in our hearts—it's not just the music. He's looking for heart expressions that will manifest themselves in songs."[1] Many can sing or play instruments well, but not all are able to "create a place" as Kenoly urges. Most of us are able to discern between a good, but routine, worship service and one in which the activity of the Holy Spirit rises above the usual. Tim Hughes, another popular worship leader, writes, "Our worship needs to be Spirit led; in fact, I would go so far as to say that the Holy Spirit should be our worship leader. Therefore, leading worship is not just a case of throwing a few favorite songs together. If we go to God on our own terms, not His, we can miss out on the Holy Spirit's plan for a meeting."[2]

Here is my definition of this gift: "The gift of leading worship is the special ability that God gives to certain members of the Body of Christ to accurately discern the heart of God for a particular public worship service, to draw others into an intimate experience of God during the worship time, and to allow the Holy Spirit to change directions and emphases as the service progresses."[3]

Please note that both deliverance and leading worship are biblical *activities*, but they are not named as *gifts* per se in the Bible. Since the lists of gifts are open-ended, I believe that it is appropriate to add certain gifts, such as deliverance and leading worship. I also think we should add the gift of intercession, which I will discuss in detail shortly. I don't believe, however, that we'll really understand the gift of intercession if we cannot tell the difference between spiritual gifts and Christian roles. Let me explain.

Gifts Versus Roles

Every spiritual gift, like every member of the human body, is itself in the minority. Think of it. More members of your body are *not* fingers than are fingers. More are *not* lungs than are lungs. Likewise in the church. More members are *not* apostles than are apostles. More are *not* prophets than prophets. More are *not* administrators than administrators. We could go down the whole list of spiritual gifts in the same way.

Although relatively few Christians have any particular one of the 28 spiritual gifts in the list, all Christians, without exception, have roles that parallel most of the gifts. For example, while all believers do not have the *gift* of evangelist, all do have the *role* of being a witness for Christ and leading unbelievers to the Lord. Not all have the *gift* of giving, but all do have the *role* of generously giving tithes and offerings and alms and firstfruits. Not all have the *gift* of healing, but all do have the *role* of laying on of hands and praying for the sick. Again, as you can see, we could continue down the list of gifts.

This distinction is extremely important, and I have been disappointed at how few Christian leaders help their people understand it. We all do many, many things in our churches and in the workplace to fulfill the multiple roles that God has given us. However, there are certain things that we do with a higher and more consistent degree of power and effectiveness. These are the areas in which we would want to begin to discover our spiritual gifts.

Now let me focus more specifically on the ministry of intercession and draw the distinctions between the role and the gift.

Intercession as a Christian Role

Intercession, as I mentioned in the last chapter, is a specific kind of prayer. It means standing in the gap, usually on behalf of another person or group of people or a cause. Jesus Himself is described as an intercessor. Paul tells us that He is at the right hand of God, where He "makes intercession for us" (Rom. 8:34). The Holy Spirit also "makes intercession for the saints according to the will of God" (Rom. 8:27). While the Son and the Holy Spirit are standing in the gap for us, the Father is never mentioned as an intercessor.

Why? Because He is always the One to whom the intercession is being made.

On the human level, Paul characterizes himself as an intercessor when he says to the Romans, "Without ceasing I make mention of you always in my prayers" (Rom. 1:9).

Before developing the idea of intercession as a spiritual *gift*, I want to make it clear that intercession is a *role* expected of every faithful believer. I say this even though it is self-evident that every Christian we know prays for or intercedes for other people. They may not use the language, but they stand in the gap. Paul says to Timothy, "Therefore I exhort first of all that supplications, prayers, intercessions, and giving of thanks be made for all men" (1 Tim. 2:1). James admonishes, "Confess your trespasses to one another, and pray for one another, that you may be healed" (Jas. 5:16).

Every one of us should be interceding for others—and most of us undoubtedly should be doing it much more than we do. If I am honest, I will have to admit that although I do intercede for others, I probably do not intercede enough. I need to intercede more for my spouse, my children, my grandchildren, my extended family, my colleagues in ministry, my apostolic alignment, and my friends, both saved and unsaved.

At the bare minimum, the Christian life should be characterized by at least one designated time each day for prayer, including intercession. How long this daily time should be I will discuss later on. In the meantime, my point is simply that the daily rule I am advocating is not just for some Christians, but for all of them. Let me repeat: Intercession is a universal Christian *role*.

Intercession as a Spiritual Gift

As I have been saying, intercession is not one of the 25 spiritual gifts mentioned specifically as gifts in the New Testament. However, like the gifts of deliverance and leading worship, I believe it should be added to the list. Whenever I share this with pastors, they almost invariably tell me that in their congregations are certain people whom they and others openly recognize as having a special prayer ministry, over and above that of the average believer. This is an early clue that they might have the gift of intercession.

What exactly is this gift? Here is my answer: "The gift of intercession is the special ability that God gives to certain members of the Body of Christ to pray for extended periods of time on a regular basis, experience a special intimacy with God, and see frequent and specific answers to their prayers to a degree much greater than that which is expected of the average Christian."[4]

The field research that I have been able to do over the years has indicated these special characteristics of people with the gift of intercession:

- They pray longer. One hour per day is the minimum I have encountered; more typically, they pray two to five hours per day.
- They pray with more intensity. For many, their prayer time is often an emotional experience involving both laughter and tears.
- They achieve a sense of intimacy with God—a familiarity that allows them to hear from God and see through God's eyes for any circumstances He chooses.
- They have a greater faith to know that they are praying in God's will, and that the will of God is going to be accomplished.
- They enjoy prayer more and receive more personal satisfaction from their prayer times.
- They see more frequent and dramatic answers to their prayers. This raises their faith and provides more fuel for the fires of intercession that burn within them.
- They are acutely aware of hearing clearly and directly from God. Many have both the gift of intercession and

the gift of prophecy. I have observed a significant overlap between these two gifts.

How Many Have the Gift?

How many members of an average congregation have the gift of intercession? The answer to this question is not fully known. Certain denominations or theological traditions may have more recognized intercessors than others. I say "recognized" because I am convinced that there are many people with the gift of intercession in our churches who have not yet discovered their own gift or begun to use it effectively, because their church environment is not conducive to releasing this gift. However, I believe the trend toward encouraging people to discover and activate their gift of intercession has been accelerating in America over the past few years.

One of my prayers for this book is that God will use it to change the spiritual environment so that more and more churches across denominational lines will aggressively promote the ministry of intercession on all levels, but especially for Christian leaders.

Earlier I mentioned the Pareto Principle and the law of the vital few. While in most cases the vital few comprise 20 percent of the particular group in question, the numbers are a little different when it comes to the gift of intercession. With intercession, the percentage is much smaller—smaller even than I myself thought it would be at first. My field research has driven me to the conclusion that even in congregations that are aware of the gift of intercession and give it a good profile in church life, this "vital few" will number somewhere around 5 or 10 percent. For years, including at the time I was first writing this book, I taught the "120 Fellowship" adult Sunday School class at Lake Avenue Church. We had around 100 active members, which, by the way, is larger than the average congregation in the United States (only 75 members). As you would imagine, I did a survey of this class; when I did, I found that seven of my class members had the gift of intercession. Yes, that is 7 percent, right between 5 and 10 percent.

Women as Intercessors

When I first compiled the list of my seven class members who had
the gift of intercession, guess what? All seven were women! Since
then I have made it a point to examine prayer ministries across denominational and cultural lines, and I have found that around 80
percent of believers who have the gift of intercession are female.
I think you will agree that this fact is worth looking into.

First, let me say that I do not believe any of the 28 spiritual gifts
is gender-exclusive—meaning that only men have it or only women
have it. On the other hand, it is obvious that some are gender-biased.
For example, women tend to show a higher occurrence of the gift
of pastor (this does not necessarily relate to ordained ministry or
running a church, but rather to pastoral caregiving). More women
have the gift of evangelist than men. At the same time, men tend
to show a higher occurrence of the gift of leadership (as in serving
as senior pastor of a congregation) and the gift of teacher. The two
genders might be more equal in the occurrence of other gifts, such
as exhortation or service.

The gift of intercession is clearly biased toward women. Why
should this be? Psychological profiles in general have shown women
to be more intuitional and men to be more rational. That's where we
get the phrase "women's intuition." Some intercessors themselves
have suggested that a woman's biological function of conception,
gestation and the travail of giving birth might have something to
do with it. Some intense periods of intercession have been described
as "travail." Mothers know even better than could the apostle Paul
the full meaning of his words "My little children, for whom I labor
in birth again until Christ is formed in you" (Gal. 4:19).

None of what I am saying here should be interpreted as exclud-
ing men. Some of the most powerful intercessors I have met are
men. I know many males with the gift of intercession, and through
the years I have not found any who harbor even a shade of resentment that they happen to be in the minority in their prayer ministries. Even though men may be in the minority, a disproportionate

number of them are the leaders of their prayer groups or ministries. Some pastors I know restrict their personal prayer partners to men only.

Later on I will sketch a profile of personal intercessors, but meanwhile I think the lyrics of a song titled "Prayer Warrior," by the outstanding Gospel group Heirloom, describe them beautifully:

> You may see her in the grocery with her children
> Or in the city nine to five each working day.
> She's a mother or a teacher or a woman all alone
> But she's something else entirely when she prays.
> We don't see her lonely nights of intercession
> Or the tears she sheds with every whispered prayer.
> We may not see the secret things hidden in her heart
> But the eyes of God are watching her with care.
> She's a prayer warrior down on her knees
> Wrestling with powers and principalities
> Standing in the gap for others
> For her sisters and her brothers
> Reaching heaven with her heart.[5]

The Office of Intercessor

It's one thing to have been given the gift of intercession by God; it's another thing to be commissioned to the *office* of intercessor by the Body of Christ. Gifts are received by grace, but offices are gained by works. What works? The visible manifestations of the fruit of the particular gift. Once the church recognizes that an individual believer has a certain gift, and the fruit of that gift has been manifested for sufficient time, and if the person passes the leadership character tests of 1 Timothy 3, that person can be formally commissioned into the corresponding office.

Most of us are accustomed to this process as it relates to the office of pastor. It is common for a person with the gift of pastor to be examined by an ordination committee and then ordained. The ordination committee does not confer the gift; rather, it recognizes that God has given the gift of pastor to the individual, as attested by their works. Some churches are now also commissioning apostles, prophets, evangelists and teachers, as well as workplace ministers. We likewise recognize the office of intercessor and commission qualified individuals accordingly.

When seeking to commission intercessors, we need to be sensitive to the fact that not every believer with the gift of intercession will accept the office. Why? Because along with the public recognition comes a higher level of responsibility, accountability, and therefore commitment. Some do not desire this. Also, intercessors will be the first to know that once they have accepted the office, they will become subject to a higher intensity of spiritual attack. But some are willing to take the risk, and as a result awesome new spiritual power is being released in churches, communities and workplace environments across the country.

Ministries of Intercession

First Corinthians 12 gives us the most detailed explanation of spiritual gifts in the Bible. One of the things this passage does is distinguish *gifts* from *ministries* from *activities*. It says that there are "diversities of gifts" (v. 4), "differences of ministries" (v. 5), and "diversities of activities" (v. 6). Each of these areas is specifically attributed to the working of God.

I take this to mean that different people who have the same spiritual *gift* might have different *ministries* assigned to them by God. For example, among those with the *gift* of evangelist, some may have a *ministry* of personal evangelism, while others may have a *ministry* of public evangelism.

Taking this one step further, some with the same *ministry* might have different *activities* assigned to them by God. Let's look at those who have the *ministry* of public evangelism as an example.

Some may be called to the *activity* of citywide crusades, while others may be called to the *activity* of church-based evangelism. Of the latter, some may have the *activity* of going from church to church, while others may be evangelistically gifted pastors who evangelize primarily from one pulpit.

This principle will apply to any spiritual gift, including the gift of intercession. How many ministries can be associated with the gift of intercession? When I first wrote this book, I was able to distinguish 4 of them. But later, Tommi Femrite, one of Doris's and my long-time personal prayer partners, was able to add 8 more to come up with a list of 12 types of intercessors. For the purposes of this book, I will stick to my original 4, with the recommendation that you also read Tommi's book to learn about the others.[6] The ministries I identified are (1) General Intercessors, (2) Crisis Intercessors, (3) Personal Intercessors, and (4) Warfare Intercessors. Some intercessors may fit into more than one category, while others may just concentrate on one of them.

1. *General Intercessors* (Tommi calls these "List Intercessors"). These intercessors will spend long hours praying over prayer lists, prayer guides, and any number of miscellaneous prayer requests given to them. Many churches collect slips of paper with prayer requests on Sunday mornings. General intercessors will faithfully pray for these requests during the week. Ask a General Intercessor to pray for something and you can rest assured it will be well prayed for.

2. *Crisis Intercessors.* A crisis intercessor prays almost exclusively on assignment, with assignments coming directly from the Father. They do not respond well to random requests for prayer from individual people, and most of them would be bored to tears with a prayer list. Tommi admits, "In all honesty, praying from a list is sheer misery for me."[7] Crisis intercessors like to go into their

prayer time with worship and praise, draw near to the Father, and hear from Him what they are to pray for. Some assignments are short term, while others are long term. Once God tells them to pray through a crisis situation, they will hang on to that situation like a bulldog until it is resolved or until God "releases" them from the assignment.

My friend Christy Graham says, "I fit mostly into the category of 'Crisis Intercessor.' The Lord shows me specific concerns and people for which to intercede. Usually, but not always, it is for a specific time of crisis that I carry the burden to pray." Christy says that frequently the Lord supernaturally gives a specific insight about a particular person's need, and she adds, "Along with the information comes a burden to pray and a sense of responsibility."[8]

Many years ago, Christy was given a long-standing and indefinite assignment to pray for Albania. When I first heard this, I felt sorry for poor Christy—because there appeared to be no chance whatsoever that Albania, the world's most anti-Christian nation at the time, would ever open to the gospel. However, the whole world stood in awe as things changed in 1991 and Albania opened! The angels may have rejoiced, but none more than Christy, whose prayers—along with those of many others—played a part in opening that nation for God's kingdom.

I think that Paul's friend Epaphras may have been a Crisis Intercessor. Paul wrote to the Colossians that Epaphras was "always laboring fervently for you in prayers" (Col. 4:12). He added that Epaphras had "great zeal" not only for the Colossians, but also for those in Laodicea and Hierapolis (see v. 13). That sounds like the kind of prayer assignments that intercessors such as Christy Graham regularly receive from God.

3. *Personal Intercessors.* Some intercessors receive a special calling to pray on a regular and intense basis for a

specific person or persons. Usually these are Christian leaders both in the church and in the workplace. This whole book is an in-depth examination of personal intercession. Biblically, as I have already mentioned, I believe that Euodia and Syntyche of the Philippian church were Paul's Personal Intercessors (see Phil. 4:2-3) and that Mary the mother of John Mark was Peter's Personal Intercessor (see Acts 12:12).

4. *Warfare Intercessors.* Some intercessors are called especially to engage the enemy in high-level, or strategic-level, spiritual warfare. This is an advanced form of intercession and is by far the most demanding and potentially dangerous type. It is true that Crisis Intercessors and Personal Intercessors frequently find themselves doing spiritual warfare, but Warfare Intercessors are like the Church's Navy Seals. God has blessed me with several Warfare Intercessors on my personal prayer team.[9]

Discovering Your Gift of Intercession

Undoubtedly some will be wondering how to know whether or not they actually have the gift of intercession. It is important to keep in mind that if you do have the gift of intercession, it is only because God has graciously chosen to give it to you. It is not one of those skills, such as dancing ballet or playing baseball, that you can decide to acquire through hard work and persistence. God gives the gift; your responsibility is to discover whether or not you have it.

The process of discovering whether you have the gift of intercession is the same as it is with any of the 27 other spiritual gifts. I have elaborated on this process in some detail in my book *Your Spiritual Gifts Can Help Your Church Grow*, so I will only summarize it here. There are five steps you need to take to see if you have this or any other gift.

1. Explore the Possibilities.

This step is simply to make sure that what you are looking for is truly a spiritual gift. Helps, for example, is a spiritual gift, while humor is not. I am convinced that intercession is a spiritual gift. All believers must pray and intercede, but some obviously have a gift and ministry of intercession far above the ordinary.

A very useful tool for exploring the possibilities and helping set the direction for the next four steps is the best-selling questionnaire *Finding Your Spiritual Gifts*. This survey includes 135 questions aimed at uncovering which spiritual gifts, including the gift of intercession, might be yours. It does not profess to give you final answers, but it does pinpoint specific gifts for you to pray about and to keep in mind as you go through this discernment process. You will find the questionnaire in the back of the book I just mentioned, *Your Spiritual Gifts Can Help Your Church Grow*, and also in the smaller version of that book, *Discover Your Spiritual Gifts*. However, if you are able to get the workbook, *Finding Your Spiritual Gifts*, you will find it much easier to grade.

2. Experiment with the Gift.

If you suspect that you might have the gift, try interceding as much and in as many ways as you possibly can. This experimentation should be long-term and undertaken in a serious manner. Ask God to show you through the process whether or not you have the gift. If your gift turns out not to be intercession, move on and discover what your gift or gifts are. And still continue as a faithful pray-er.

3. Examine Your Feelings.

If you have a gift of intercession, you will grow in your desire to pray. The Bible says, "It is God who works in you both to *will* and to do for His good pleasure" (Phil. 2:13, emphasis added). If you find after a period of time that intercession is hard work or drudgery and you do not look forward to doing it, chances are you do not have the gift. But if praying for relatively extended periods of time is your joy and delight, begin to believe that you have the gift. Cindy Jacobs, a proven intercessor, expresses it well: "People who have the gift of intercession love to pray. They would rather not do anything else. When people ask me how long I pray in a day, I reply, 'As much as possible!'" When she disconnects her telephones and spends whole days in prayer, "Those days are pure bliss to me!"[10]

4. Evaluate Your Effectiveness.

Part and parcel of receiving a spiritual gift is to enjoy supernatural help from the Holy Spirit in order to accomplish whatever the gift was designed to do. Are you hearing clearly from God? Are your prayers being answered with more than average regularity? Is faith easy for you? Do you sense special power being released through your prayers? If so, you may well have the gift of intercession.

5. Expect Confirmation from the Body.

I like the story that Graham Fitzpatrick, a confirmed intercessor, tells about how he discovered his gift. He had read about the renowned Father Nash, who would intercede for hours on behalf of the legendary evangelist Charles Finney. Fitzpatrick found that it gave him great peace and joy to picture himself interceding for hours also. But he was immature in the things of the Lord and had no way of knowing for sure if all this was an inner witness of the Holy Spirit or not. So he did the right thing and asked God to show him.

Sure enough, the Holy Spirit spoke clearly to two other members of the Body of Christ about him. According to Fitzpatrick, one man he had just met for the first time "said to me that God wanted me to be an intercessor for other people." Then a woman who knew Fitzpatrick, but was unaware of his yearning for intercession, also told him that he was to serve God as an intercessor. His conclusion: "God used these two Christians to confirm what

I thought was His speaking to me, really was Him and wasn't my own imagination or a demon."[11]

If you have a spiritual gift and begin to use it, you can expect that other members of the Body of Christ will confirm to you that it is authentic.

Which raises one final point: If you do go through this process, and you (as well as others around you) recognize that you actually have the spiritual gift of intercession, do not be reluctant to acknowledge to others that you have the gift. Do not engage in false humility. You are not "bragging" about being an intercessor any more than Billy Graham would brag about being an evangelist or than your pastor brags about being a pastor. It is part of good stewardship to thank God for the talent He has given you, to hold yourself accountable to others, and to use it to bear fruit thirty-, sixty- and one hundredfold.

Reflection Questions

1. Discuss whether you think it is possible for God to give any spiritual gifts to believers today that are not mentioned specifically as gifts in the New Testament.
2. Explain in your own words the difference between spiritual gifts and Christian roles.
3. Why do you think it is that more women than men have been given the spiritual gift of intercession?
4. Do you know anyone who would fit into one or more of the four ministries of intercession mentioned in this chapter? Name them and discuss their ministry.
5. Are you one to whom God has given a gift of intercession? Discuss the reasons behind your answer.

WHY PASTORS NEED INTERCESSION

Please let me explain why I focus on pastors, especially in these next two chapters, but also in the book in general. I feel I need to mention this because of the sharp learning curve I have been on since the first edition of *Prayer Shield* was released in 1992.

A sharp learning curve inevitably involves paradigm shifts, to which I am no stranger. One of my newest books is *This Changes Everything*, in which I look back on almost 60 years of ordained ministry and find that over time I underwent 17 significant paradigm shifts. I decided to write a chapter on each one. I personally feel that shifting paradigms can be healthy; after all, Romans 12:2 tells us to "be transformed *by the renewing of your mind*" (emphasis added). Two of the chapters in *This Changes Everything* that represent some of the most important things I have learned since the first edition of *Prayer Shield* are "From Ministry in the Church to Ministry in the Workplace" and "From Society as One Mass to the Seven Mountains."

The basic meaning of "church" (Greek *ekklesia*) in the New Testament is "the people of God." This includes the people of God meeting together with one another, most often on Sunday, as well as the same people of God living out their faith wherever they happen to find themselves during the rest of the week, particularly in the workplace. Some would describe these two realities as "the church gathered" and "the church scattered." My preference for terminology is the "nuclear church" (our traditional way of picturing the church—with a congregation, a church building, a pastor, etc.) and the "extended church" (the church in the workplace). Our erroneous tendency in the past has been to relegate all true "ministry" to the nuclear church. But we are now recognizing that what God assigns His people to do in the workplace is just as valid a form of Christian ministry. This change in thinking, as you can imagine, involves a major paradigm shift.

Most of us have always believed that God's people are supposed to be salt and light in order to bring the values of God's kingdom to whatever location in which God has placed them. We dream of our society being transformed for the better. However, we can plan and strategize for this mission much more effectively if we picture society as being molded by "Seven Mountains": religion, family, education, media, government, arts and entertainment, and business. (You may remember these mountains from the Introduction to this edition.) Going by Ephesians 4:11, we know that God gives apostles, prophets, evangelists, pastors and teachers to lead the Church. But generally we think that these leaders are only for the nuclear church in the Religion Mountain, not for the extended church in the other six mountains. Our new paradigm suggests, however, that the leaders God has given to the Church will be found in all seven mountains, not just the Religion Mountain.

You can imagine how these new paradigms would change my perspective regarding intercession for Christian leaders. When I first wrote *Prayer Shield*, I thought that all valid Christian ministry was supposed to be done in the Religion Mountain and that the key players were pastors. At that time I knew virtually nothing about the ministry of apostles and prophets in the Church today. That does not give me an *excuse* for focusing so strongly on pastors in this book, but it does offer an *explanation* as to why I did so.

Where does this leave me with regard to the second edition of *Prayer Shield*? Realistically speaking, I am firmly embedded in the Religion Mountain. I do not have the personal insights or experience to deal adequately with the other six mountains. However, God has raised up Tommi Femrite, an intercessor who has been a key part of Doris's and my personal prayer shield for many years, to help fill in this gap. Tommi has developed a for-profit company called AIN (Apostolic Intercessors Network) designed to provide professional-level intercession for Christian leaders in all seven mountains. Her book, *Invading the Seven Mountains with Intercession*, is a vital companion volume to *Prayer Shield*. If you like my book, you will love hers!

Because I did my seminal research for this book on pastors, and because pastors will continue to be important players in Christian leadership circles, I will continue to focus on them, hoping that we all recognize that the principles I apply to pastors and "other Christian leaders" include minsters in the workplace as well as apostles and prophets.

The Cost of Being a Pastor

I am convinced that most church members have little or no appreciation of the personal cost of being a pastor. They, of course, know what their pastor looks like and sounds like on the *outside*, but they have little more idea of what is happening to their pastor on the *inside* than they would have about what is happening on the inside of their digital watch or their GPS.

By way of warning, I am intending to be quite frank in this chapter about what actually goes on inside of pastors and other Christian leaders, but please keep in mind that nothing I say is to be taken as criticizing them any more than a doctor diagnosing hepatitis or high blood pressure would be criticizing the patient. The purpose is healing. I believe not only that intercession can be *therapeutic* for the spiritual and emotional maladies of pastors, but also, much more importantly, that powerful intercession can be *preventive*.

Pastors Are More Beat Up Than You Think!

The pastor most church members see, know and relate to week after week conforms to a well-established social standard. Certain things are expected of a pastor—things that are not necessarily expected of an auto mechanic or a nurse or a lawyer. The title "Reverend" carries strong social connotations.

Church members tend to take all of this for granted, but pastors can't! It does not come naturally. Pastors constantly work to project a suitable public image for a clergy person, even those of the younger generation who wear jeans with their shirt tails out and try to be "hip." The pastors church members see week in and week out are on their best behavior. They are appropriately dressed, they display a cheerful disposition, they are affirming, they control their temper, they watch their language, they treat their spouses well, they are unselfish, they work hard, they keep smiling, and they hope their people see them as Christlike. But this is only part of the story.

Pastors are also human beings. They are saved by grace and are sanctified no differently than the auto mechanic or the nurse or the lawyer in their congregation is. Many, if not most, pastors will actually remind their people of this in their sermons from time to time.

For example, when a pastor warns in a sermon against a certain temptation, he or she might say, "I am not exempting myself. I am as human as you are. This can be as much of a temptation for me as it is for you." The people usually acknowledge this as an affirmation of humility, but they relegate it to rhetoric. They do not really believe it, mainly because they do not want to. Part of their own Christian well-being depends on following a pastoral leader whom they regard as somewhat higher on the scale of piety and spiritual attainment than they will likely ever be. With society's help, they often put their pastor on a spiritual pedestal.

Most pastors and other Christian leaders are not trying to be hypocrites. They generally know very well that on the inside they may not be all their congregations expect them to be. Their spouses know this also, but few others do. Consequently, pastors are often caught in a bind. They sense God's calling on their lives to serve as pastor, and they know that they cannot do an effective job as pastor if they do not outwardly conform to their congregation's expectations. But, at the same time, how do they handle what is going on inside?

Pastors Need Help

To put it simply, *most* pastors *need help*. When I was teaching at Fuller Seminary, I would meet and interact with hundreds of pastors, year in and year out. Even though I did not necessarily relate to them as a counselor or as a pastor to pastors, I found that, across denominational lines, many were beat up spiritually, emotionally, and sometimes physically.

Where can struggling pastors go for help? They are reluctant to approach any of their church members. Word could too easily leak out that the pastor is failing the congregation by not meeting their expectations. Pastors in the same denomination are usually on friendly terms with one another but tend to be somewhat distrustful at the deeper levels. A professional counselor? What would church members think if they knew? Pastors of other churches in the same community are likely prospects for help but are themselves frequently overburdened and unavailable. Beyond those circles, most pastors simply run out of meaningful relationships.

Happily, there are some exceptions. I have encountered pastors who do not fit this bleak picture I have been painting. Some of these pastors experience little internal conflict because deep down they actually are what they are expected to be, emotionally and spiritually. Others are not, but they have found their own sources of help and are managing their situations well. I wish I could report that these two groups make up the majority of pastors, but I am afraid I cannot. Without wanting to oversimplify a terribly complex situation, I do want to point out that Satan has many pastors just where he wants them. They are vulnerable to his attacks, and consequently they are not able to fulfill all of their God-given destiny.

An Epidemic of Falling Pastors

In recent years, an alarming number of pastors have dropped out of vocational ministry for two main reasons: pastoral burnout and sexual immorality. This has included some very high-profile leaders. The numbers have reached epidemic proportions.

I cannot recall hearing much about pastoral burnout during the early years of my ministry. I'm sure it existed, but not to the degree that we see it today. The situation I have been describing, resulting in pastors being so beat up, makes it quite easy to understand why so much burnout would occur. The enemy knows this well and has become quite astute at raising pastoral frustration—through feelings of inadequacy, hypocrisy, guilt and low self-esteem—to such levels that selling insurance or painting houses could seem to some like a more attractive way to make a living.

Literature on causes of and remedies for pastoral burnout is now readily available. Good time-management training is helping many to avoid it. Even so, I believe that the powers of darkness are perpetually active in attempting to block the effectiveness of pastors. If this is correct, strong and organized intercession for pastors has enormous potential for counteracting this opposition.

Pastoral Indiscretion

Satan may win some significant battles by causing pastoral burnout, but he inflicts immeasurably more damage to the cause of Christ when he influences a pastor or other Christian leader to fall through sexual immorality while they are in the ministry. The bad news is that, according to a survey by the clergy journal Leadership, 12 percent of practicing pastors have committed adultery.[1] The good news is that 88 percent have not!

Surveys like this would have seemed scandalous a couple of generations ago. Back then, Elmer Gantry was not looked upon as a realistic prototype of anything but a miniscule fringe of American clergy. Now the picture has changed. For a time, I dropped news clippings on the subject into a file folder. When I opened up the folder, I was appalled to find 26 media reports of sexual immorality on the part of high-profile clergy, almost half of whom I knew personally!

I remember a front-page article in the *Los Angeles Times* that carried the headline "Sex Abuse Cases Rock the Clergy: Disclosures of misconduct—a problem hidden for years—are on the rise." A nationally syndicated column by the Associated Press announced, "Sex scandals in higher ranks shake up hierarchies."

Evangelicals, charismatics, fundamentalists, Pentecostals, liberals and Roman Catholics all wish they could point their fingers at the others, but none is exempt. Here is a mainline bishop known widely as an "evangelical." Here is a seminary professor. Here is a televangelist. Here is a civil rights folk hero. Here is a megachurch pastor. Here is a best-selling author. Here is a missions leader. Here is a liberation theologian. Here is a black pastor; there is a white one. Here is a 25-year-old; there is a 60-year-old. Here is a pastor from Massachusetts; there is a pastor from Arizona. Where is it going to stop?

Reporting this makes me upset! I am not upset at my friends who have fallen—even though I, along with the rest of the Body of Christ, have been saddened. Rather, I am angry at the enemy—who, I feel, is getting away with far too much these days. We unfortunately have failed to recognize the intensity of the spiritual battle we are fighting.

The enemy knows that pastors are beat up; he knows they are vulnerable, and he attacks them at their weakest point. I do not mean to imply that those who have fallen are not themselves guilty and do not have character flaws that need to be repaired through humility, repentance, reconciliation, deliverance, inner healing, restoration and holiness. But I do hope and pray that we will quickly learn how to use our spiritual weapons more effectively in putting a stop to these blatant and all-too-successful attacks of the devil. Intercessors provide a major weapon to help us win this battle.

Pastors Need Intercession

As I have said, every Christian needs intercession. The little girl in the sixth grade first learning what AIDS means needs intercession. The long-haul truck driver trying to witness to his friends at the truck stop about Jesus needs intercession. The Christian stockbroker wrestling with the ethics of that last transaction needs intercession. The mother homeschooling three kids needs intercession. I do not want to ignore the need for more consistent ministries of intercession across the board.

However, I do want to argue that pastors and other Christian leaders, such as apostles and prophets, need intercession more than ordinary members of the Body of Christ. This statement may sound strange and even arrogant at first, but let me propose five reasons why I believe it to be true.

1. Pastors Have More Responsibility and Accountability.

Most of us Christian leaders get chills up and down our spines when we read James 3:1: "My brethren, let not many of you become teachers, knowing that we shall receive a stricter judgment."

All Christians will come before the judgment seat of Christ, but pastors and other leaders have been forewarned that there is a divine double standard—one standard for "teachers" and other leaders, and a less strict standard for everyone else.

In other words, in the eyes of God, a given sin is worse for a pastor to commit than it is for others. The first problem, of course, is the sin itself, and that may be the same for everyone. But the second problem is the violation of the *office,* which is even more serious. When someone has been equipped by God to fill an office such as pastor, teacher or apostle, and has been recognized as such by the Christian community, it is a grievous offense to break that trust.

Let's face it, accepting a position of leadership in the Christian world means running a risk. Sin becomes more dangerous than ever before. This is one good reason why pastors have a greater need for intercession.

2. Pastors Are More Subject to Temptation.

Make no mistake about it: The higher up you go on the ladder of Christian leadership, the higher you go on Satan's hit list. The devil is characterized as a roaring lion seeking whom he may devour. If he has a choice, he will devour a leader before he will devour anyone else. And he will use every weapon in his arsenal to do it.

What are his weapons?

First, Satan uses the *world* (see Eph. 2:1-2). He tempts pastors with greed and power and pride. Money and power team up with sex as some of the strongest lures for ministers. The secular media have recently uncovered some of the greed among Christian leaders, which others of us have not particularly wanted to face. We probably have not seen the end of this. The love of money is a root of evil (see 1 Tim. 6:10), and Satan has been getting in through that gate more than some have suspected.

Satan also uses the *flesh* (see Eph. 2:2-3). Enough has already been said about illicit sex. Keep in mind as well that Satan all too often perverts the soul with pornography. Other ministers are tempted to fall into gluttony or alcohol or substance abuse—all traps set by the flesh.

Finally, Satan uses the *devil* (see 1 Pet. 5:8; John 13:27). This means demonization, spells, curses and incantations. To imagine that pastors are only subject to the world and the flesh, but not the devil, is in itself a clear satanic deception.

It is true that every Christian is subject to all of the above. However, Satan is more specific, persistent and intentional when it comes to pastors and other leaders.

3. Pastors Are More Often Targets of Warfare.

It has now become known that over the last several years, Satanists, witches, New Agers, occult practitioners, shamans, spiritists and other servants of darkness have entered into an evil covenant to pray to Satan for the breakdown of marriages of pastors and other Christian leaders. The spiritual warfare has intensified.

In my book *Warfare Prayer*, I distinguish three levels of spiritual warfare: (1) ground-level spiritual warfare, which is ordinary deliverance ministry; (2) occult-level spiritual warfare, which involves spells and curses by spiritual practitioners of darkness; and (3) strategic-level spiritual warfare, which deals with territorial principalities and powers. The three levels interact with one another to varying degrees, but the warfare is different in each case. Here I am speaking of occult-level spiritual warfare. Special kinds of intercessors, particularly the warfare intercessors I mentioned in the last chapter, are needed to deal with this most effectively. And other intercessors are needed as backup.

Spiritual warfare targeting Christian leaders is such a critical issue that I want to be sure we do not think it is a figment of someone's imagination. I have personal correspondence from two respected Christian leaders who have had firsthand exposure to this phenomenon. These leaders can help us understand the reality of the struggle we have reluctantly been drawn into.

The first report comes from John Vaughn of the International Church Research Center in Bolivar, Missouri. I have known and respected John for years. The scenario described in this report is an airplane flight from Detroit to Boston, where Vaughan was to do a pastors' seminar.

John had not conversed with or paid much attention to the man in the seat next to him until he saw the man bow his head and move his lips as if praying. When he finished, John casually said, "Are you a Christian?" The man had no way of knowing that Vaughan himself was a Christian, a Baptist pastor and a university professor.

He seemed shocked by the question and replied, "Oh, no. You have me all wrong. I'm not a Christian; I'm actually a satanist!"

John then asked him what he was praying for as a satanist.

The man said, "Do you really want to know?"

When John affirmed that he did, the satanist replied, "My primary attention is directed toward the fall of Christian pastors and their families living in New England." He then asked John what he was planning to do in Boston.

John reports, "After a brief conversation about my ministry and its purposes for the kingdom of God, he indicated that he needed to return to his work!"

This encounter made John realize just how essential intercession for pastors really is. Did Christians take time to pray for their pastors in New England that day? Whose prayer was answered—the Christians' or the satanist's?

Award-Winning Satanists

Bill McRae is the chancellor of Ontario Theological Seminary in Canada. Previously he pastored the North Park Community Chapel in London, Ontario.

McRae reports that while he was a pastor, "It was brought to our attention that a group of satanists who worshiped in a church situation within London had committed themselves to pray to Satan for the elimination of a number of our evangelical leaders in the city through marriage and family breakdown. During that summer the cell group in London was honored at a particular satanist convention for being so effective and successful during that year."

Why did they win the award? McRae says, "In the course of the previous year they had succeeded through their prayers to Satan in eliminating five of our very significant leading men from pastoral ministries through immorality and marriage breakdown!"

He goes on to say that he was deeply involved with one of the pastors who was going through this nightmarish and disgraceful fall from Christian ministry. "We were very much aware of the desperate need for prayer, but I must frankly confess none of us was quite as alert to the reality of the satanic warfare we were fighting until it was over."

McRae also tells of a group of his friends who went into a restaurant in London, where they observed an obvious prayer meeting being conducted in a corner booth. Curious, they approached the booth and introduced themselves as fellow Christians. One of the group members quickly corrected them, explaining that they belonged to the Church of Satan in London. They added that they had been praying that night for the destruction of a certain pastor. McRae says, "They mentioned his name, and he is a very good friend of mine in one of the leading churches in London. It once again brought home to me the dark reality of the satanic battle in which we are engaged."

Spirits of Lust

Apparently, one of Satan's favorite tactics is to assign powerful spirits of lust to target Christian leaders. Some of the closest contact I have had with pastors came during a two-week Doctor of Ministry course that I taught at Fuller Seminary twice a year. In one of the course sessions, I made a comment that at first sounded very humorous. In the classroom, I had more than 50 pastors from across denominational lines and from many different parts of the country. It was an advanced course, so they had all studied with me before and knew me well. On the first day of class, I told my students, as I usually did, that their two weeks would not only be a time of learning new material, but that God would also use it as an opportunity for the pastors to minister to one another and draw closer to God.

I then mentioned that my wife, Doris, who was my administrative assistant and to whom many of them had talked on the phone, had a powerful deliverance ministry and that she usually focused on pastors and other Christian leaders. I casually told them that she had a particularly effective track record of delivering pastors from demonic spirits of lust. Then I went ahead and said, "So if any of you has a problem with lust, go see my wife!"

I made the comment so spontaneously and naively that we all burst out in laughter. But then what happened? No fewer than six of the pastors made appointments with Doris for deliverance sessions! They went home with a new lease on life. Several later wrote or called, telling Doris how different and more enjoyable life was since they had been delivered from those foul spirits. One wrote, "For the first time since we have been married, my wife and I can now pray together!"

Nothing said here should cause us to suppose that demonization relieves pastors or others of moral responsibility. The opening for the activity of a spirit of lust, more often than not, can be traced to "the lust of the flesh" (1 John 2:16) or to sin that needs to be identified and dealt with biblically. Part and parcel of the deliverance process is typically (1) a personal recognition of and hatred for the sin; (2) a sincere desire to get rid of it; (3) a courageous first step of faith—like making an appointment to see Doris; and (4) confession of the sin, often in considerable detail.

This fulfills James 5:16: "Confess your trespasses to one another, and pray for one another, that you may be healed." In this case the healing is spiritual. Upon sincere repentance, the root sin is forgiven by God's grace and the legal grounds allowing the demonic activity are effectively removed. Once this is accomplished, the demonic spirit can be dismissed rather easily. Without sincere humility and repentance, however, the demon either stays or soon returns with reinforcements.

I have dealt with this subject of spiritual warfare in quite some detail here for two reasons. First, I want to make sure we understand that it is real. While it is not the only cause, it is a frequent contributor to so many pastors falling into sexual immorality.

Second, I want us to understand that there is a remedy, namely the power of God released through effective intercession. My desire in this book is to explain clearly and as thoroughly as possible how the power of intercession can be released for repairing damage already done by the enemy and preventing further occurrences.

4. Pastors Have More Influence over Others.

The fourth reason why pastors and other Christian leaders need intercession more than other believers is that, by the very nature of their ministry, they have more influence over others. If a pastor falls, more people are hurt and set back in their spiritual lives than if other individuals fall. The ripple effect can be incredibly devastating. Strong Christians are crushed by the hypocrisy and betrayal they feel. Weak Christians can use the pastor's behavior as a license to do likewise.

Not only does the fall of a pastor injure an untold number of individuals, but it also directly influences churches. My study of church growth has always focused strongly on the pastor, because we have accumulated empirical evidence that the pastor is the major institutional factor for determining the growth or non-growth of a local church. Satan hates churches that glorify God and extend God's kingdom, and he does what he can to bring them down. No wonder he focuses his sights on pastors!

But in the plan of God, the gates of hell will not prevail against the advance of the Church (see Matt. 16:18). Intercession for pastors is a major stimulus to release God's plan for a glorious Bride of Christ.

5. Pastors Have More Visibility.

Because pastors are up front, they are constantly subject to gossip and criticism. When church members have Sunday dinner, the pastor and the sermon of the morning are frequent topics of conversation.

People talk about the good but also the bad. The pastor is closely observed—and this is no secret. Just knowing it places a difficult burden on pastors, and they need supernatural help to handle the situation well. Intercession opens the way for them to receive this help.

Intercession Improves Ministry

It is not a simple matter to conduct the type of research necessary to prove or disprove the power of prayer. However, Nancy Pfaff, an intercessor and church growth consultant, has attempted it. As a project in graduate school, she designed a research instrument and surveyed 130 pastors, evangelists and missionaries. Intercessors trained through Iverna Tompkins Ministry in Scottsdale, Arizona, each agreed to pray 15 minutes a day, for an entire year, for one of the 130 leaders.

What happened? About 89 percent of those surveyed indicated that the prayer had caused a positive change in their ministry effectiveness. They reported more power in the use of their spiritual gifts, a higher level of positive response to their ministry, more discernment and wisdom from God, increased wholeness and completeness in Christ, improved attitudes, more evidence of the fruit of the Spirit, better personal prayer lives, and heightened leadership skills.

Pfaff's research also uncovered several important variables. She found that daily prayer for leaders was more effective than weekly or monthly payer. Also, persistent prayer was shown to be important. Pfaff reports, "Where intercessors stopped praying for their assigned leader after a few weeks, the leaders indicated no positive changes in their lives and ministries during that year."[2]

Intercession also appears to aid church growth. Pfaff found that of 109 pastors covered by intercessory payer, 60 percent indicated that their churches grew. For example, a pastor from Pennsylvania testified that over the period of the 12-month prayer experiment, his church grew from 15 to more than 600 members. No wonder

Pfaff says, "There exists a tremendous reservoir of untapped prayer power in every church which can be affirmed, trained and deployed to see the lost won, the apathetic revived, the backslider restored and the committed made more effective."[3]

Back when the well-known Evangelism Explosion program was moving out from Coral Ridge Presbyterian Church in Fort Lauderdale, Florida, and spreading across the country, Archie Parrish, who was then serving as director of the program, made an important discovery. Even though things seemed to be working well, he introduced a new innovation. He had each participating church enlist two church members who were not in the Evangelism Explosion program to pray for each Evangelism Explosion worker, especially on the Tuesday nights when the program was in operation. The evangelist was responsible to report back to his or her intercessors each week. Archie was excited to discover that when intercessors prayed, the number of professions of faith in cooperating churches doubled!

Pastors and other Christian leaders are needy people. However, they are God's chosen ones to move His kingdom forward. Faithful and intelligent intercession can release them to be all God wants them to be.

Reflection Questions

1. This chapter suggests that many pastors are "beat up." Why do you think this could be true? Give some examples that you know about.
2. What is it that makes a pastor or other Christian leader more responsible for moral behavior than the average believer?
3. Distinguish between the three levels of spiritual warfare mentioned in this chapter, giving examples of each from your own knowledge or experience if possible.
4. Discuss the possibility of evil spirits causing lust in a pastor's life. In this case, should the pastor blame the spirits rather than taking personal responsibility for his or her behavior?

5. If intercession will improve your pastor's ministry, what suggestions could you make for action steps to release more prayer on your pastor's behalf?

SECRETS OF PASTORS' PRAYER LIVES

With admirable transparency, Baptist pastor Mark Littleton says, "Parishioners would never dream it, but there is a segment of the ecclesiastical nobility—myself included—for whom personal worship (a.k.a. 'devotions,' 'quiet time,' 'QT') has been a struggle. First, it's finding the minutes. Those phone calls in the morning always seem to foul up your communion with God. Or maybe it's the kids. Or the sweet smell of coffee wafting from the kitchen."[1]

Many church members take for granted that their pastor, as their spiritual leader, spends considerable quality time alone with God on a regular basis. They love their church and they love their pastor—and they naturally assume that their pastor is a "man of God" or a "woman of God." Little do they suspect that one of the higher items on the list of pastoral frustrations is the gap between the prayer life that pastors know they need (and desire to have and frequently preach about) and what they're actually able to make happen in real life.

One pastor says, "Like most busy people, I am plagued by pressures, deadlines, phone calls, 'emergencies,' and on and on. Sometimes I think the devil works overtime just to keep me from prayer." Knowing what I know about the devil, I think the last sentence might be an understatement.

How Much Do Pastors Pray?

Several surveys have been done on the prayer life of pastors. Before I report on them, however, I want to be sure you realize that I may not be talking about your pastor when I cite averages. Your pastor might well be above average—possibly even far above average. While this would be nice, the odds are that you do not really know offhand where your pastor stands, because few church members do. Not that your pastor *intends* that his or her prayer life should be kept a secret, but in most cases it is. Ask any church member who comes out the door on Sunday morning.

When *Leadership Journal* conducted a survey of 125 pastors' prayer lives, the findings indicated that the majority of pastors felt that they were virtually without human support in their devotional lives. By some invisible mutual agreement, the pastor's prayer life seemed to be an inappropriate topic of conversation in the parish.

One of the pastors said, "I get the feeling others don't think my personal devotional life is important." In the years that he had been on the staff of this particular church, he said, "Not one person (including the senior pastor) has asked me about the health of my personal faith. I feel totally unsupported in this aspect of my life."[2] The majority of the 125 pastors surveyed harbored similar feelings.

I personally conducted a survey of 572 American pastors who had enrolled in my Doctor of Ministry Advanced Church Growth course at Fuller Seminary over some years. The pastors crossed regional, age and denominational lines. I wanted to find out just how much time a day ordinary pastors spent in actual prayer. In the survey, I was not counting Bible study, reading devotional books, listening to worship DVDs, or other components of a fully rounded devotional life. I was dealing only with prayer.

In my sample, I found:

- 57 percent prayed less than 20 minutes per day.
- 34 percent prayed between 20 minutes and 1 hour per day.

- 9 percent prayed 1 hour or more per day.
- The average daily prayer time was 22 minutes.

I did not find significant variation by age, although pastors over 60 years of age seemed to pray a little less than the others. I found no regional variation. I did find what may turn out to be a significant theological variation in that pastors who perceived themselves as Pentecostals/charismatics reported praying for longer periods of time than did those who saw themselves as evangelicals or liberals. I will get back to this later on, when I discuss the issue of prayer and church growth.

The *Leadership Journal* survey to which I referred earlier likewise found that pastors prayed 22 minutes per day, by and large, so this figure seems to be consistent. But my survey also showed that 28 percent—more than 1 out of 4 pastors—prayed less than 10 minutes per day!

What can we compare this to? A Gallup poll found that 88 percent of all American adults pray to God. Of those who do pray, 58 percent of them pray every day.[3] But unfortunately, this survey did not report the amount of time spent in prayer.

Clergy Prayer in Other Nations

I personally was able to conduct on-site surveys in four other nations. I found that:

- Australian pastors average 23 minutes per day in prayer.
- New Zealand pastors average 30 minutes per day.
- Japanese pastors average 44 minutes per day.
- Korean pastors average 90 minutes per day.

In South Korea, another survey I saw showed that 83 percent of pastors across denominational lines pray one hour or more every day. One out of three prays two hours or more. One of my close friends, Pastor Sundo Kim, whose Kwang Lim Methodist Church at the time was reported to be the largest Methodist church in the world (more than 5,000 members in 1990), has a prayer closet built into his study. When I looked inside, I saw only a pillow on the floor for kneeling, a Bible on a low stand, a cross and a picture or two on the wall, and nothing else. Kim told me that he spends at least an hour and a half a day in that closet.

That hour and a half, by the way, is over and above the hour or more he spends every single morning leading his church's predawn prayer meeting and the time he spends in other prayer groups and in one-on-one praying throughout the day. Like many other Korean pastors, Kim also has a motel-like bedroom and bath connected to his study, because he ordinarily spends all of Saturday night there fasting and praying for Sunday's ministry. His prayer habits would be typical for Korean pastors.

Do Pastors Pray Enough?

Getting back to America, for many years I spent a good bit of time teaching pastors on the subject of prayer. Whenever I would bring up the subject, they would admit frankly to me and to one another in the classroom that they knew their prayer lives were not all they should be. Although some did have first-rate personal prayer habits, and some were happy with their 22 minutes per day, the great majority wanted to pray more than they did.

Pastor Mark Littleton remarks that he does his best to stick to a consistent prayer life through "sick and sin," as he puts it. His exasperation surfaces when he says, "You try it with the television on. With the television off. At home. At your office. Under the beech trees in the park. In bed. Out of bed. You go for a week straight and don't miss once. The next week you miss seven for seven."[4]

Books and sermons on prayer feature a standard list of heroes of the faith who have led extraordinary prayer lives. John Wesley rose at 4:00 each morning and spent 2 hours per day in prayer. Martin Luther said, "I have so much to do today, I will have to spend the first three hours in prayer, or the devil will get the victory." Adoniram Judson disciplined himself to withdraw and pray seven times each day. John Welch of Scotland, the companion of John Knox, committed 8 to 10 hours per day to prayer.

The list goes on. John Hyde of India prayed so much that he earned the nickname "Praying Hyde." Henry Martyn, David Brainerd, George Muller, Robert Murray McCheyne, Hudson Taylor, George Fox and some others habitually make this roster of all-star intercessors. All of these spiritual giants accomplished great things for God—things most of today's pastors would love to duplicate. But if their performance in ministry depends on sustaining that kind of a prayer life, most pastors I know simply despair.

No one puts it more clearly than Mark Littleton once again. He admits that reading about these super pray-ers "nearly wipes you out." As holy as David Brainerd might have been, Littleton says, "you get a bit tired of him lying in the snow, praying for six hours, and getting up wet. Not from the snow, though. From the sweat."[5]

Richard Foster speaks for me, and probably for numbers of others, when he says, "Many of us. . . are discouraged rather than challenged by such examples."[6] I can still remember reading the biography of Praying Hyde when I was a young Christian. I had become so discouraged by the time I finished that I think it might have been the last Christian biography I ever read!

But enough lamenting about the current state of affairs. Few will deny that pastors and other Christian leaders, both in the church and in the workplace, need better prayer lives. The driving question is, What can we do about it? I think the answer is twofold:

- First, pastors and other leaders need to pray more. (When I used to say this in my Doctor of Ministry classes, some of the pastors would jokingly respond that they were going to ask for their tuition back!)

- Second, pastors and other leaders need to learn to receive intercession.

If I may, I will elaborate a bit on the first part of the solution here, and then use the rest of the book to deal with the second part.

Pastors Need to Pray More

One of the reasons I am not going to deal with many of the specific whys and hows of praying more is that the majority of books on prayer already deal with them. We do not lack resources in this area. The average Christian bookstore's section on prayer contains many excellent titles. True, these may not be specifically aimed at the prayer life of pastors or other Christian leaders, but the general principles of a disciplined and rewarding prayer life apply across the board.

As I have perused the literature on prayer, however, I have noticed that four issues in particular need elaboration because they are dealt with either not at all or, at least in my opinion, inadequately. I refer to (1) the issue of time, (2) the issue of gift projection, (3) the issue of church growth, and (4) the issue of personal ministry. Let's look at each of these issues individually.

The Issue of Time

How much time should be spent in prayer? How important is the time factor?

I think that a fruitful way to approach the answers to these questions would be to explore the essence of prayer. When all the trimmings are peeled away, prayer must be seen basically as a relationship. It is our individual, personal relationship with God the Father. Our ability to have this relationship was provided by Jesus Christ on the cross. He shed His blood for the remission of sin—the sin that separated us from God. Through our faith in Jesus, our sin is forgiven and our fellowship with God is restored. Only after all this has happened does prayer take its true form. We now love God because He first loved us and paid the price to bring us to Himself.

Prayer—especially prayer accompanied by worship—is the chief way we express our love to God, and the chief way we receive God's love for us. It is the most exquisite expression of our personal relationship. If we can understand that through prayer our divine love affair with the Father is cultivated, we can more accurately assess the value of time spent in prayer. Everything we know about human relationships tells us that devoting time to being together is essential if the relationship is to grow.

The Minimum Daily Requirement

First things first, prayer time must be regular. A consensus among Christian leaders who have specialized in matters of prayer, devotional life, spirituality and Christian discipleship is that there should be a time of prayer every day. No pastor or other Christian leader should let a single day go by without some specific time set aside from other activities for talking to God.

I believe it is helpful for us to develop habits of praying while we are taking a shower, driving a car, standing in line, riding a bus, or washing the dishes. But when I speak of a daily prayer time, I mean programming specific blocks of time just for God into our calendars, day-timers and cell phones. Dual tasking will not cut it. Not a day should go by without specific prayer time on any Christian's schedule, but especially on a leader's schedule.

To say that on some days our schedule is too busy to fit in a time with God is to make a decision with pretty negative implications. No one has any more or less time than anyone else—24 hours per day. How each of us decides to use that time boils down to our personal priorities. Pastors in general have more ultimate control over their daily schedules than the majority of humans who work in other professions.

I realize that some pastors, and apostles as well, feel that their schedule controls them. This, however, is due to faulty time management, not to the nature of the pastoral or apostolic vocation. If we cannot find daily time with God, our relationship with Him is obviously not one of our highest personal priorities. If this is true, spiritual disaster could be right around the corner.

"I Love You!"

Some time ago, I was conversing with a friend about our families. He said, "After so many years of marriage there are things you begin to take for granted. For instance, I don't tell my wife I love her every day—she knows it and has known it for years." At the time, I did not feel that it was appropriate for me to reply, but in my mind I was saying, *I do! I tell my wife I love her every day and we don't get tired of it.*

Even though Doris and I have been married for more than 60 years, I try to tell her explicitly at least once a day that I love her. In my mind, some things in life are too important to take for granted—such as my love relationship with my wife. This applies to my love relationship with God as well. I intentionally try to keep both among my highest priorities every day.

I can imagine that some may be saying we should not be so legalistic. God is a God of grace, not of law. Therefore, He will maintain the relationship between us on His initiative, whether or not we perform by scheduling a daily prayer time. I certainly agree with a theology of the grace of God, and I affirm with others that chronic legalism should not be characteristic of our personal Christian lifestyles. However, I will go on to say that on this particular issue of time with God, if I err I would far rather err on the side of consecrated legalism than on the side of excessive leniency.

I again like the way Mark Littleton puts it: "I have to ask myself the question: Are all the activities that scream for my time and attention in twentieth-century America really essential? Am I missing the burning bush for trying to keep the lawn cut?"[7]

Time Must Be Sufficient

Having a regular daily prayer time is the first and most essential component of a pastor's or other leader's personal prayer life. A second important consideration is the amount of time spent in each prayer session. I personally find myself less legalistic about the duration factor than I am about the consistency factor, although I can quite confidently state that as a general principle, *the more time spent daily in* prayer *the better.*

I have found that almost all pastors I know who have a true heart for deepening their personal relationship with God agree with this. The arguments I have heard against it cause me to be suspicious of the proponents of those arguments. They too often sound like rationalizations designed to justify a slipshod devotional life that unfortunately has become a lifestyle.

What are the time ranges? The 22-minute-a-day average should probably be considered the minimum in our particular (non-Korean!) cultural context. John Welch's eight hours or Luther's three hours or Wesley's two hours per day are probably far beyond any realistic proposal for today's American pastors.

As a starter, I would recommend that if you are praying less than 22 minutes a day, you make that your first goal.

Then where do we go from there? I have been strongly influenced by Larry Lea's book *Could You Not Tarry One Hour?* I think Lea has served as a principal contextualizer of the Korean prayer movement into our American society. He makes a compelling case for aiming toward one hour of prayer per day.

Another authority on intercession from whom I have learned a great deal is Mike Bickle of the International House of Prayer in Kansas City. Mike agrees with Larry on the one hour per day goal. The *Leadership* survey of 125 pastors that I have previously cited asked them, "How much time per day do you think you *should* spend in prayer? More than half (53 percent) said 30 to 60 minutes and about half of the others (24 percent) said more than one hour."[8]

In light of this survey, I suggest that pastors and other Christian leaders agree that our norm for daily prayer time should be 22 minutes to one hour.

But what about the quality of our time with God? Isn't *quality* more important than *quantity*?

Contrary to what some may think, I believe it is advisable to start with quantity rather than attempting to start with quality in daily prayer time. First, program the time. The quality will usually follow. Mike Bickle says that when you first spend 60 minutes in a prayer time, you should not be surprised if you come out of it with something like 5 minutes that you consider quality time. Keep it up and those 5 minutes will become 15, then 30, then more. The ideal, of course, is to end up with both quantity and quality, not one or the other.

Our current society, characterized by two working parents, high divorce rates and single-parent families, has reduced the quantity of time that parents typically spend with their children. To help compensate, many have developed a concept of "quality time" with the kids. However, psychological studies on the children have now shown that no "quality" of time can substitute for quantity of time with children. One of the high priorities of these children who are now becoming parents themselves is to return to a lifestyle in which they can spend "quantity time" with their children. I believe the same principle applies to our time with our heavenly Father.

The Delicate Issue of Gift Projection

I purposely refrain from saying very much about the syndrome of gift projection in my seminars or in my classes—mainly because it can be painful for some leaders to discover that they have unintentionally been practicing it. I deal with it in detail in my book *Your Spiritual Gifts Can Help Your Church Grow*, and many readers have commented that it was one of the most helpful sections for them. It helped them get rid of some false guilt complexes they had been nurturing.

As I was in the process of researching for this book, I felt that God was saying quite clearly to me that I should include a brief section on gift projection here also. I am praying that what I have to say about gift projection in relation to intercessory prayer will not be offensive, even though I know that it may run against the grain of some of the things we tend to believe. On the positive side, I also know that it will free up many people to be what God wants them to be instead of trying to be what other people might want them to be.

So, what is gift projection?

Some people who customarily minister powerfully in a certain area do so simply because God has chosen to give them the necessary spiritual gift. However, for a number of reasons, they fail to recognize that they have that particular gift. Consequently they think that everyone who is a Christian believer and who is in proper relationship with God could and should be doing the same thing they are doing. They attempt to project their gift onto others. It does not occur to them that God may have chosen *not* to give this particular gift to different members of the Body of Christ, but that He has instead given them other gifts that they should be concentrating on.

Much of this lack of understanding is rooted in the notion, held by many classical Pentecostals and others, that all the spiritual gifts are given to all believers who have been duly filled with the Holy Spirit. Most of those who hold this position limit the number of available spiritual gifts to the 9 found in the beginning of 1 Corinthians 12 rather than regarding the whole list of 28 that I mentioned in chapter 2 as equally legitimate spiritual gifts. This starting point quite easily leads to gift projection.

Inflicting False Guilt

The message that often comes through is, "I am an ordinary Christian just like you. God has not given me any special privileges. What

He is doing through me God also wants to do through you. If you really want to, you can do the same powerful ministry that I do; you just have to believe that Jesus is the same yesterday, today and forever. I urge you to make up your mind to do whatever is necessary so that with the help of God you can also do the ministry that I am doing."

The unintended result of projecting your spiritual gift onto those who have been given different gifts is false guilt, discouragement and frustration. The guilt is false because people who do not have the particular spiritual gift in question try their best to do what the gifted ones do, but they fail. So where do they assign the blame?

- Am I not spiritual enough?
- Do I have unconfessed sin in my life?
- Am I unworthy of God's love?
- Is God mad at me?
- Do I not pray enough?
- If only I were as consecrated to God as this spiritual giant I am listening to, I would be able to match their effectiveness in ministry!

I will refrain from mentioning specific names at this point, although I could list many who are household names in the Christian community who regularly project the gift of evangelism, the gift of prophecy, the gift of hospitality, the gift of healing, the gift of word of knowledge, the gift of discernment of spirits, the gift of mercy, the gift of faith, the missionary gift, and many others. These leaders habitually make others who do not have their gifts feel guilty about it.

How about the gift of intercession? This is one of the most projected gifts. The historical heroes of the faith such as Praying Hyde, John Welch, David Brainerd, Adoniram Judson and others obviously had the gift of intercession. Do we all need to be exactly like them? Of course not! By way of illustration, I am thinking of a particular megachurch pastor whom I know but will not name. He tells of spending three to five hours each day in prayer. Referring to another pastor, I have actually heard this megachurch pastor say in public, "If Reverend so-and-so decided to pray as much as I do each day, his church would be as large as mine!" What a senseless and heartless putdown!

Those with the gift of intercession who expect others to be more like them would do well to review Paul's teaching in 1 Corinthians 12–14. Do all have the gift of healing? Obviously not. Do all work miracles? Obviously not. Do all have a gift of administration? Obviously not. Do all have the gift of helps? Obviously not. Do all have the gift of intercession? Obviously not. This is made clear in 1 Corinthians 12:27-30. If we all had the same gift (for example, the gift of intercession), the body would turn out not to be a body at all, but just a single part—perhaps an eye. Paul explains the problem with this scenario: "If the whole body were an eye, where would be the hearing?" Then he goes on to say, "Now God has set the members, each one of them, in the body just as He pleased" (1 Cor. 12:17-18).

Let me reiterate what I said in chapter 2: We must keep in mind the difference between spiritual gifts and Christian roles. Specific *gifts* are given by God to certain believers and not to others, according to His design. However, roles should be characteristic of all believers. They are not gifts; they are simply Christian qualities. For example, certain believers have the gift of healing, but every believer has the role of laying hands on the sick and praying for healing. These are two different things. The same is true with intercession. Some, but not all, have the spiritual gift of intercession. However, we all have a role of prayer and intercession. Parents do not need a special spiritual gift in order to intercede for their children—it is their role to do so. As we have seen, few pastors have the gift of intercession. Nevertheless they should set aside 22 minutes to one hour daily to exercise their role of prayer and intercession (without feeling guilty about not praying more). This does not require a spiritual gift—it is their role.

The Issue of Church Growth

Given that researching and teaching on church growth have been a significant part of my career, I would not want to omit a brief section on the subject. Fortunately, as we saw in chapter 3, some researchers, such as Nancy Pfaff and Archie Parrish, have begun to explore the direct relationship of prayer to evangelism and the growth or non-growth of churches. While this is going on, we can surmise a strong *indirect* relationship simply by looking at the biblical record. Ever since Jesus said, "I will build My church" (Matt. 16:18), we have known that churches grow by the power of God. And prayer releases the power of God here on earth. Undoubtedly the extraordinary growth of churches we are seeing today in most parts of the world can be attributed, at least in part, to prayer.

Having said that, let's take a brief look at what some researchers are actually finding. Kirk Hadaway, a respected sociologist of religion, conducted a study of churches that were plateaued as compared to other churches that were experiencing breakout growth. Hadaway found that "71 percent of breakout churches report an increased emphasis on prayer over the past several years as compared to only 40 percent of churches which continue on the plateau."[9]

Similarly, leading church-growth expert Thom Rainer identified 576 Southern Baptist churches characterized by "effective evangelism." He found that "nearly 70 percent of the churches rated prayer as a *major* factor in their evangelistic success" (emphasis his).[10] Rainer goes on to say, "Therefore, we conclude, with conviction, that most evangelistically growing churches are also praying churches."[11]

Still, not much in the literature on prayer or the literature on church growth shows how the connection is actually made. This means that we still need to develop action plans that can activate the power of prayer to help churches grow more effectively than they have been doing. I was part of conducting some field experiments in Argentina (reported in *Warfare Prayer*) that indicated that strategic-level intercession and spiritual warfare opened the way for dramatic church growth. I included several other case studies in *Churches That Pray*. But admittedly all these fall short of what sociologists would consider an empirical study.

Meanwhile, the survey of 572 American pastors that I have previously mentioned might not have provided scientific conclusions, but it can give us some interesting clues. When we examine the dynamic growth of churches worldwide, it is evident that the greatest growth is coming within the Pentecostal/charismatic tradition. Statistics indicate the following:

- In 1900 there were 981,000 Pentecostals/charismatics.
- In 1970 there were 62,685,000.
- In 2000 there were 459,840,000.
- In 2013 there were 628,186,000 and adding 42,000 per day.[12]

Although I do not pretend to be a professional historian, I think the following statement has a good bit of merit: In all of human history, there has never been a nonpolitical, nonmilitaristic, voluntary human movement that has grown as rapidly as the Pentecostal/charismatic movement has grown over the last 50 years.

How does this relate to my survey? As I pointed out earlier, the one significant variable I found in the amount of time that American pastors spent in prayer had to do with Pentecostal/charismatic pastors. When the survey results were broken down by theological traditions, we saw the following:

- Liberal pastors averaged 18 minutes per day.
- Evangelical pastors averaged 17 minutes per day.
- Pentecostal/charismatic pastors averaged 46 minutes per day.

America is one of the many nations where Pentecostal/charismatic churches are outgrowing all others by leaps and bounds. Could the fact that the pastors of these churches set aside more than twice the amount of time for daily prayer as do pastors of slower growing churches have anything to do with their vigorous rate of growth? It does seem quite likely, doesn't it?

If so, this would point to another measureable benefit that could be received as more and more pastors begin pushing those 22 minutes of daily prayer toward one hour.

A Word of Encouragement

I am praying that this chapter, which I know has been very frank and honest, will be used by God to draw thousands of pastors, apostles, marketplace ministers and other leaders closer to Him than they have been before. I am confident He will do that.

A word of encouragement along these lines came from a pastor with whom I had lunch soon after I did the survey. He later shared that the most significant part of our conversation for him was discovering what I was learning about prayer. He wrote, "After hearing about the average time in prayer for pastors of 22 minutes, and what God was doing in response to the prayers of His people around the world, I have determined to spend two hours a day in prayer." Since beginning this, he reports, "I have sensed the presence and power of the Holy Spirit in a new way in my life and ministry."

Most pastors and other leaders whom I know agree that they need to improve their prayer lives. A first step is to personally pray more regularly and for longer periods of time. Fortunately, they can also learn to receive the intercession of others. The rest of this book will deal with receiving personal intercession.

As pastors and leaders we tend to be activists. We can easily identify with Joshua out there fighting the battle of Rephidim. What we need to learn more about is how God can bring into our lives and ministries gifted people who, as Moses did for Joshua, will spend hours and days in the presence of God on our behalf so that His power can flow liberally to give us the effectiveness we desire in our personal ministry.

Reflection Questions

1. Does it come as a shock to discover that even pastors have a difficult time maintaining a quality prayer life? Why or why not?
2. Do you think it is too legalistic to suggest that Christians find a specific time each and every day to pray?
3. How do you feel about the suggestion that the first step in improving one's prayer life is to concentrate on the quantity of time, assuming that quality will eventually follow?
4. "Gift projection" may be a rather difficult concept to grasp at first. Discuss it with others until you feel you understand it. Why is this practice so dangerous?
5. Do you know how much your pastor prays each day? Do you feel that this should be considered private information? Why or why not?

RECEIVING PERSONAL INTERCESSION

The statement I am about to make will probably sound puzzling at first:

My personal prayer *life is first class! My personal* prayer *habits are mediocre.*

The puzzle, of course, lies in how I can have it both ways. How can I struggle with mediocre personal prayer habits and still enjoy a first-class prayer life?

My answer is quite straightforward: I have learned how to receive personal intercession, and I consider this intercession part of my personal prayer life.

Mediocre Prayer Habits?

When I admit that my personal prayer habits are mediocre, that's the bad news. The good news is that they are better than they used to be!

I did not grow up in a Christian home where church, Sunday School, prayer and the Bible were a normal part of life. It was only after I left home that I was born again and became a committed

Christian. Some of my early Christian training came through InterVarsity Christian Fellowship, where I learned that part of the expected behavior pattern of a believer was to have a daily "quiet time." The InterVarsity leaders explained that I was supposed to read the Bible and pray every day. That sounded good—so I began to do it. Because I have always been able to exercise a certain amount of self-discipline, I maintained this daily pattern for years. Throughout seminary and my three terms on the mission field in Bolivia, I had a standard quiet time, day in and day out.

If anyone had asked me at one of those moments when I was in a particularly transparent mood, I would have admitted that I did the quiet time, purely and simply, because I considered it my duty. I also brushed my teeth, took my vitamins, got my hair cut, and changed my underwear regularly. It was all part of what respectable Christians did. Although I cannot recall any especially good feeling while I was doing those things, the whole process felt good just because I had accomplished what I was supposed to do.

Then, at 40 years of age, I went through a mid-career change from a field missionary in Bolivia to a Fuller Seminary professor in Pasadena, California. This also undoubtedly precipitated a classic mid-life crisis, although I am not much for self-administered psychoanalysis. But part of what I was going through was that one day, after being back in the United States for a couple of years, I suddenly decided that I was wasting my time with this dry, routine Bible-reading and prayer. So I quit! For a number of years, I just got up, had my breakfast, and went to work without blocking off any of the time for God that I advocated so strongly in the last chapter.

Bad choice! As the next few years went by, I gradually became convinced that I was *not* better off without a regular prayer time. My seminary classes were going well, my outside ministry with church leaders was quite well received, and my career appeared to be advancing satisfactorily. However, I always managed to find myself in the midst of excessive amounts of turmoil and polemics.

Moving forward seemed to be a constant uphill struggle. Soon I began suffering from high blood pressure and recurring severe headaches. Because I was only marginally in touch with the Lord, I didn't even realize that I had fallen into the habit of striving in the flesh rather than resting in the Spirit. Imagine that on the part of a respected seminary professor!

I'm sure that it was the persistent gentle prodding of the Holy Spirit that began to bring me back to my senses and helped me recognize that I'd better resume a regular daily time with God. But knowing that I was supposed to do it and actually putting it into practice were two different things. My problem was that I wanted to start something new—not fall back into the dry routine I had endured for years.

Fortunately, things changed!

The *Reader's Digest* Sermon

It was my pastor, Paul Cedar, who came to the rescue. One Sunday morning in the early 1980s, he told the congregation at Lake Avenue Church that he was going to do something that he had never done before and probably would never do again. As part of his morning message on prayer, he was going to read word-for-word an entire article from *The Reader's Digest*. Sure enough, it turned out to be an article on spending time with God each day.

I am sure that many others among the 2,000-plus in the congregation that day were touched by the *Reader's Digest* sermon, but none more profoundly than me. I immediately knew that God was speaking to me, but I still worried about how I was going to implement what I knew I would have to do sooner or later. At the end of the sermon, Paul Cedar did me an enormous favor.

He said, "I know that some of you have not been having a regular quiet time, and my prayer is that you will start up this week. I'm not going to ask for a show of hands, but I am going to ask that in your heart you make a promise to me as your pastor. I'm going to ask you to promise me that you will give five minutes a day to God, starting this week."

Five minutes? I honestly do not know what I would have done if he had said 30 minutes or an hour, but I said in my heart, Paul, *I can handle 5 minutes per day. You have my promise that I will do it.*

And I did. The next morning I spent 5 very special minutes with God. The 5 soon became 10. Then 15. The time kept increasing. Then it plateaued—at about 22 minutes, which, as I reported in the last chapter, turned out to be the average among U.S. pastors. True, 22 minutes might not be all that much, but it is a whole lot better than zero!

Tarrying One Hour

I was comfortably rolling along at about 22 minutes of prayer a day when I started seriously researching the whole field of prayer in 1987. One of the early books I read was Larry Lea's *Could You Not Tarry One Hour?* In it he makes such a persuasive case for praying one hour per day that I resolved to set that as my goal. Now, many years later, I can say I have left the 22 minutes behind. I pray more than 30 minutes on most days, and occasionally more than 40. But one hour? It is still a life goal, and I may make it someday. But not yet. One hour is a really long time for prayer! At least, it is in *my* mind.

I will never forget the first time I prayed for one hour. This was back in the 1970s, when I was still in my prayerless season. I had been going to South Korea from time to time to research church growth, and had become personal friends with David Yonggi Cho, pastor of the Yoido Full Gospel Church, the world's largest congregation. On one of my visits, Cho offered to take me to the famous Yoido Church Prayer Mountain.

I had never visited the prayer mountain, so I jumped at the chance, looking forward to a personal tour. When we arrived, I began wondering when the tour would begin. However, Cho—of all things—simply said, "Now, let's pray!" Pray? I would have preferred walking around and taking pictures of others who were praying, but naturally I kept my thoughts to myself. Then he added, "We really don't have much time. Let's pray this afternoon for only one hour!"

I wanted to be a good sport, so I sat there on the floor of the huge chapel (Korean style) and started to pray. I prayed for what felt like quite a long time, and then I looked at my watch. I thought my watch had stopped! That turned out to be one of the longest hours I can remember spending. Time went faster when my wife was in labor!

The Lord's Prayer

Larry Lea seems to understand that people like me need special help to extend their prayer time. So in his book he makes a suggestion (which I have since discovered has a long history in Christian tradition) of structuring personal prayer times around the Lord's Prayer. This works well for me, because *praying* the Lord's Prayer, as opposed to simply *saying* the Lord's Prayer, provides a ready-made structure to cover everything one could possibly need to pray about at one time.

Structure is important to me because I have a melancholy personality. I am happiest when things are in order. When I pray, sometimes my mind wanders and I get off track. At other times I may find myself snoozing. But no matter what the distraction of the moment might be, the Lord's Prayer helps me know exactly where to pick up when I get my mind back where it belongs.

So much for my mediocre personal prayer habits. I keep trying to get better, but I'm an old dog now and not exceptionally good at learning new tricks. Meanwhile, I still affirm that I have a first-class prayer life because I add to my personal prayer the prayers of my intercessors. As I have said, I actually believe that the prayers of my intercessors constitute a real and vital part of my personal prayer life.

Discovering Intercession

I began to discover the power of personal intercession soon after I started teaching my Sunday School class, the 120 Fellowship of Lake Avenue Church, in 1982. This was not premeditated, but simply an outcome of the spiritual chemistry of the situation.

I had never doubted the authority of Scripture; therefore I could not doubt the power of prayer. However, it took a good bit of time before I really began to understand what was happening in this new class. For the first time that I could recall, I found myself in the midst of a group of believers who were support- ing me and my ministry through powerful intercessory prayer. It was a fascinating experience!

Not that others who had supported us on the mission field and elsewhere were not praying Christians. However, some of those with whom I was now associating obviously had a level of contact with the invisible world that I knew very little about.

I began to get clues as to what was happening when I noticed a new pattern forming. On an infrequent but fairly regular basis, people would approach me in the pastors' seminars that I was conducting across the country, and they would say words to this effect: "Peter, I heard you x number of years ago, and now I'm hearing you again. Your ministry has an obvious depth and qual- ity that it didn't have before. What is making the difference?"

At first I politely shrugged off the comments as undue flat- tery. But I began hearing the same thing often enough to make me do some evaluation. What was happening? I honestly had to admit that there was, in fact, increased spiritual power in my teaching. I had logged enough experience with audiences to real- ize that the words I was speaking were moving people in a more profound way than my teaching had done before. Yet, strangely enough, much of the content was not that different from a few years earlier.

I did not immediately realize that the cause of this change for the better could be intercession. But around that same time,

I happened to move into a routine of reporting the results of my previous week's ministry to the 120 Fellowship on Sunday morning and asking them to pray for my ministry the following week. Many in the class were so touched by what they heard God had done, week after week, that I began to realize they were considering *my* ministry as *their* ministry as well. They were laughing when I laughed and crying when I cried because, through their faithful intercession on my behalf, they were doing the ministry with me.

Soon I learned how to respond when people asked me why my ministry had improved. I would simply say, "I attribute it to the power of prayer through those who are now interceding for me."

This was the beginning of my experiencing the power of personal intercession. That first-hand experience soon led me into full-scale research of the biblical, theological and practical theories that would explain why personal intercession has such profound effects.

Personal Intercession Is Biblical

In chapter 1, I attempted to make a biblical case for personal intercession. I do not intend to duplicate that here, but it may be helpful just to bring up a few reminders. For example, Moses' interceding for Joshua as he fought and won the battle of Rephidim is a beautiful model. Then the apostle Paul asks for personal intercession for himself and his ministry at least five times. Euodia and Syntyche were in all likelihood two of Paul's personal prayer partners.

One day Herod decided to kill both James and Peter. He killed James, but he could not kill Peter. Why? We are told that "constant prayer was offered to God for him by the church" (Acts 12:5). The praying was done in the home of Mary, the mother of Mark, and I would not be surprised if Mary was one of Peter's personal prayer partners. Please go back to chapter 1 if you need more details showing that personal intercession is biblical.

Personal Intercession Is Underutilized

In a brochure written to stimulate prayer for missionaries, veteran missionary Robert Bowers, a medical doctor serving with SIM International, describes this all-too-familiar scenario:

"Please pray for us," a furloughing missionary says as he leaves his friend's home after a pleasant dinner.

"We will, we will!" his host replies warmly.

Bowers's comment is that this is nothing more than saying hello or good-bye—a routine social formality that carries little or no meaning. On the surface, a verbal contract was made between the two parties, confirming that this Christian family would pray for the missionary. The family's names were undoubtedly entered on the list of those who would receive the missionary's "prayer letter."

In reality, however, assuming this family to be typical of thousands of others, the actual amount of powerful, effective intercession invested on behalf of the missionary over the next four-year term of service would be practically nil. Missionaries, apostles, pastors, teachers, prophets, evangelists, denominational executives and other Christian leaders, both in the church and in the workplace, universally affirm the importance of prayer, but many still lack the know-how to actually make it happen.

As I said on the first page of the first chapter of this book: The most underutilized source of power in our churches today is intercession for Christian leaders.

Fortunately we are not starting from ground zero. Many outstanding leaders today do understand and receive powerful intercession. And the number is growing. If we look closely, we can find a number of important people from the past who attest to the power of intercession in their lives.

For example, one of today's recognized prayer leaders and students of prayer, Armin Gesswein, wrote me a letter about Frank Mangs, perhaps the greatest of the Scandinavian evangelists. Every morning, the letter said, Mangs would earnestly pray to the Lord, "Bless my intercessors today." Then Gesswein, who moves constantly among those who pray, added, "I never hear that from preachers today." I believe that Gesswein has put his finger on a real problem.

If we go back to the eighth century, we can see that Boniface, the stalwart missionary to the pagan peoples of Germany, wrote to the abbot of a monastery: "We entreat the piety of your brotherliness that we may be helped by your devout petitions... that the few seeds scattered in the furrows may spring up and multiply." And to an archbishop: "We entreat your clemency, that your piety would pray for us in our labors and dangers."[1] Boniface apparently understood the power of intercession.

Charles G. Finney, one of the most effective evangelists in American history, met a man named Daniel Nash early in his ministry. Nash eventually became Finney's personal intercessor and would frequently travel with him and pray while Finney preached. Known as "Father Nash," he gained a reputation for praying long and very loudly. It was said that when he prayed in the woods, his voice could be heard throughout the surrounding countryside.[2]

To move a bit closer to the present, visitors who tour the museum in the Billy Graham Center on the campus of Wheaton College in Illinois will see a picture of one of Billy Graham's prayer partners, Pearl Goode. Graham himself attributes much of the evangelistic power of his ministry to Goode's faithful intercession.

Five Reasons for the Neglect

No question exists in the minds of those who have experienced it: Committed, faithful intercession brings increased spiritual power to Christian ministries. Why is it, then, that so few ministers, either in the church or in the workplace, utilize it? I believe there are five important reasons for this underutilization.

1. Ignorance

I have no doubt that ignorance, pure and simple, is the number one culprit for our lack of plugging into personal intercession.

The great majority of Christian leaders have not thought about it. Although it is nothing new, either biblically or historically, it is simply absent from the day-by-day thought patterns of most Christian leaders.

The thing that first made me realize how great a role ignorance might be playing in determining personal intercession (or lack thereof) was the remarkably disproportional response I got when I started to mention the idea casually in some of my church-growth seminars designed for pastors.

While I was developing the seed thoughts for the contents of this book, I would test the waters by using 10 or 15 minutes of a two-day seminar to report what I was learning about personal intercession. An unusually large number of pastors would get back to me after the seminar, saying that what I had shared about personal intercession was more important to them than the whole rest of the seminar!

I received letter after letter like this one from a pastor in Upland, California: "Following your exhortation on personal intercession, I now have 7 prayer partners praying for me daily. I am seeing a difference in my life! Thank you." I began to realize that, more than anything else, I was rolling back a cloud of ignorance.

Some readers may remember that back in the 1980s, we in America experienced an epidemic of pastors and other leaders falling into sexual immorality. The scandals become so widespread and so public that several Christian authors began researching and writing on the subject. I made a personal collection of this material because I began to discern a trend throughout the literature reflecting our collective ignorance of the power of personal intercession.

I feel that I should mention the names of some of these authors, because their own stature and integrity in the Christian community is important to make my point. But by way of disclaimer, I want to say that I hope my motive will be properly understood. In no way am I *criticizing* these authors, many of whom are personal friends of mine. I am simply citing them because they represent all of us on this issue of ignorance.

One of the Christian classics of our generation is Richard J. Foster's *Celebration of Discipline*. Foster has been regarded as a top leader of the spirituality movement since the 1970s. He is a person of prayer. When the Jim Bakker affair became public, *Charisma* magazine asked Foster to examine the PTL crisis and analyze it for their readers. His resulting article is called "The PTL Scandal." After dealing with what happened, Foster suggests four ways to prevent such things in the future. Guess what? Not one of the four is prayer![3]

Pastor and radio personality Richard Exley wrote a book, *Perils of Power: Immorality in the Ministry*. It contains no section on prayer or personal intercession. The same is true for the book by the famous Christian psychologist Clyde M. Narramore, *Why a Christian Leader May Fall*. Likewise for the late charismatic leader Don Basham, whose book is titled *Lead Us Not into Temptation: Confronting Immorality in Ministry*. Nothing on intercession.

The two major interdenominational clergy journals in the United States each ran an issue on the subject. The *Leadership Journal* of Winter 1988 (on the general theme "Sex") included articles such as "How Common Is Pastoral Indiscretion?" "Private Sins of Public Ministry," "The War Within Continues," "Counseling the Seductive Female," "After the Affair: A Wife's Story," "Preaching on That Oh-So-Delicate Subject," and "Treating Casualties of the Revolution."

Among the better-known authors of these articles were David Semands, Archibald Hart, Bill Hybels and Chuck Smith, all leaders of peerless wisdom and integrity. But even though I looked hard for it, I could not find in all this material a single suggestion that intercessory prayer could be a preventive. A final article, by Randy Alcorn, was "Strategies to Keep from Falling." This article suggested nine preventive measures, none of which was receiving personal intercession.

Ministry Today, the second most influential clergy journal, dedicated a large part of its July/August 1990 issue to "Restoring Fallen Leaders." Here are some of its articles: "The Restoration of David Alsobrook," "Restoration by Grace," "Pastor—and Addict," "Restoring Fallen Leaders," "Picking Up After an Affair," "If Ministers Fall Can They Be Restored?" and "When a Leader Falls." In this issue I did find the power of prayer mentioned twice, but both times in the context of picking up the pieces *after* the tragedy rather than as a means of *preventing* the fall altogether.

I was happy to see that a book by Gordon MacDonald, *Rebuilding Your Broken World,* did have a section on prayer. MacDonald suggested seven "Personal Defense Initiatives," the second one being "Pay the Price of Regular Spiritual Discipline," by which he meant "the cultivation of Scripture study, intercession, meditation, and general reading on spiritual subjects."[4] All this is good, but, interestingly enough, he did not go on to mention receiving spiritual power through the intercession of others.

Though I do not wish to extend this discussion unduly, I will nevertheless update it with a reference to "7 Ways to Stop the Adultery Epidemic," a 2013 blog post by J. Lee Grady, former editor of *Charisma.*[5] I must repeat that I cite this not as a criticism of my friend Lee, who exhibits admirable personal integrity, but simply as a representative of the mindset of a huge number of Christian leaders even today. Lee was upset because over the six months prior to the posting of this article, three pastors of large churches in his hometown of Orlando, Florida, had been forced to resign their pulpits because of adultery. Lee's seven proposed ways to put a stop to this epidemic were all good. However, here is my point: It apparently did not occur to him to add an eighth suggestion, namely that Christian leaders would benefit from receiving powerful personal intercession from a dedicated prayer team.

To summarize, the radar screen of these leaders, whose stature is so widely respected, did not reveal personal intercession as one of the means for preventing pastors from falling into sexual immorality. Why? They probably never thought of it! This is what I mean when I suggest that ignorance is the number one reason we have not been using personal intercession as we should.

The notorious epidemic of falling leaders that we witnessed back in the 1980s occurred 25 or 30 years before the release of this second edition of *Prayer Shield*. I may be wrong, but I believe that immorality in the ministry has decreased considerably since then, Lee Grady's 2013 blog to the contrary notwithstanding. I have no proof, but I would like to believe that *Prayer Shield* played at least some role in helping to enable this turn for the better. If intercession helped Joshua win the battle of Rephidim, it certainly can help pastors and other Christian leaders win the battle against the flesh. This could be the proverbial ounce of prevention that is worth a pound of cure!

2. Rugged Individualism

Cultural anthropologists continually remind us Americans that we are some of the most individualistic people on earth. Many trace it to our frontier mindset. We are one of the few cultures in the world, for example, in which many young people leave home, select a mate, and then inform their parents. It's not surprising that our common notion "If I'm going to get anywhere in life, I'm going to have to pull myself up by my own bootstraps!" would carry over into our spiritual lives. This is known to be true, and to one degree or another, all of us Americans participate in it.

The good news is that our individualism encourages us to accept personal responsibility for a given task. The bad news is that we tend to ignore or despise other members of the Body of Christ—when in reality we desperately need them. We hate to admit that we might need help or that our performance is dependent on our brothers and sisters in Christ.

I will illustrate this idea by using Jimmy Swaggart as an example. It is not my usual habit to bring up names of Christian leaders who have had severe problems, but this case attracted such high public visibility for so long a time on national and international media that it is safe to assume I am not telling stories out of school. Furthermore, mutual friends have assured me that Swaggart would not object to my reiterating a lesson, for the benefit of the rest of the Body of Christ, that he himself said he learned through his experiences. I pray that this is true, because he certainly needs no additional personal pain inflicted on him at this point in time.

First of all, it is important to know something of Jimmy Swaggart's personal prayer life. He says that the Holy Spirit "impressed upon me to give a tenth of my time in prayer and in study of the Word (I don't mean studying for sermons.). That amounts to about two and a half hours a day."[6] Swaggart admits that some days he had a hard time keeping to this standard, but he nevertheless has felt a heavier anointing since setting apart this much time. Remember when I said that my research showed that the average daily prayer time for a pastor was 22 minutes? Swaggart prayed six times as much!

This means that Swaggart excelled in his personal prayer habits. He even left Larry Lea far behind! Obviously, however, it was not enough to keep him from falling into sexual immorality. Why?

E. M. Bounds points us in the right direction when he says, "The preacher is to be prayed for, the preacher is made by prayer."[7] Jimmy Swaggart had covered the first part of the formula. It was weakness in the second part that he himself cites as a source of his trouble. How do we know this?

Before the scandal broke in 1988, Swaggart had written an article for his magazine, *The Evangelist,* titled "The Lord of Breaking Through." This issue of the magazine had been printed and mailed before the bad news became public, but it was not delivered to our homes until a week after we all knew about his fall. Of course, Swaggart had known what he was doing when he wrote the article, and it sounds to me like he was trying to deal with his unfortunate spiritual condition. For example, he says:

I have always taken pride in my spiritual strength. I have believed that in my relationship with God, if He promised me something, I could have it. I can't recall, in all of my life, ever going to *anybody* and asking them for help.

Swaggart does mention that he constantly asked people to pray for him, but this is only in the sense of the missionary leaving the home after dinner and asking the host family to pray for him. It is at best a spiritual formality. He then goes on to say, quite transparently:

We are discussing personal weaknesses. Frances said to me one day, "The reason you have such difficulty in such and such an area is because of pride." That brought me up with a start. I hadn't thought about it, but I had to admit she was right.[8]

Behind this pride, of course, was that good old rugged individualism that did not feel a need for anyone's help. However, Swaggart was evidently beginning to admit his shortcomings before the scandal broke. Later he went on national television and made his memorable tearful confession. Among other things, he said:

Maybe Jimmy Swaggart has tried to live his entire life as though he were not human. And I have thought that with the Lord, knowing that He is omnipotent and omniscient, that there was nothing I could not do—and I emphasize with His help and guidance.[9]

Do you see some rugged individualism still coming through? But then comes the heart of the lesson he learned:

I think this is the reason (in my limited knowledge) that I did not find the victory I sought: because I did not seek the help of my brothers and sisters in the Lord. . . . If I had sought the help of those that loved me, with their added strength, I look back now and know that the victory would have been mine.[10]

I could not agree more. I see personal intercession as a vital activator of the immune system of the Body of Christ. To the degree we can get rid of the idea "If I am going to make it with God, I'm going to have to do it myself," we will free ourselves to look elsewhere in the Body of Christ for the God-given resources we so desperately need. Releasing God's power through intercession will go a long way toward preventing the enemy from bringing us down.

Fortunately, others are now learning the lesson. One of Swaggart's close personal friends, missionary Mark Buntain, wrote an open letter to him after the scandal became public. In it, Buntain confesses, "I never once prayed for your own life to be protected from Satan's power. . . . Oh, why was I not pleading with the Holy Spirit to not only anoint you with preaching power, but that He would keep you with His inward power?"

Buntain all but shoulders the personal responsibility for Swaggart's fall. He says to Swaggart, "I am guilty. I have failed you and failed you badly." Some will say that he overreacted, and perhaps he did. But his message is one we should all hear clearly. Serious personal intercession could have and probably would have changed this low point of contemporary Christian history.

3. Fear

The third reason personal intercession is underutilized is fear.

I must admit that there is some justification for the fear that certain pastors and other Christian leaders might have of personal intercession. They may not have given it much thought, but intuitively leaders realize that when they begin to relate to personal intercessors, they move into deeper levels of vulnerability and accountability than they have experienced before. This is not just imagination; it is a fact. Like it or not, having personal prayer partners causes your life to become much more of an open book.

I mentioned before that John Maxwell, at that time pastor of Skyline Wesleyan Church, had a team of 100 men who were committed to intercede for him and his ministry. I visited Skyline several times and got to know Dick Hausam, who had received a special assignment from God to focus his prayers on John's moral life. John was on the road about as much as an NBA basketball player. He was no more exempt from temptation than any other man in his 40s.

Just about every Sunday, Dick would approach John and say, "How did it go this week?"

John would reply, "It went real well, but I don't know how it would have gone if you hadn't prayed for me!"

This is what I mean by vulnerability and accountability. I realize that not every pastor is up to this, and fortunately such a degree of transparency is not necessarily a prerequisite for relating to personal prayer partners. Most prayer partner relationships start with considerably less personal accessibility. Some grow into it and some do not. But even those relationships that do not grow in this way end up being much better than having no prayer partners at all.

Another justification for fear stems from a common characteristic of prayer partners, particularly those with a gift of prophetic intercession. I mentioned before that there is a notable overlap between the gifts of intercession and prophecy. Intercessors frequently receive unsolicited information directly from the Lord about the pastor or leader for whom they are praying.

Experienced and discerning intercessors can be expected to know things about the pastor's life that the pastor supposes are secret. Fortunately, God does not entrust such information to intercessors unless He is sure that their level of maturity and wisdom can handle it. My own prayer partners, and others I know who pray for other leaders, assure me that God shows them things they are not at liberty to share, sometimes even with the pastors for whom they are praying.

Although this understandably can be a source of fear, we really should not be afraid of it. The intercessors have been given the information they have not to harm us personally or to harm our ministry, but to do just the opposite. They love us and desire God's best for us. Through their prayers, obstacles to the productivity of our ministry and to our personal fulfillment in Christ can be removed without our even knowing it, leaving us more liberated than we have been up to that point.

4. Spiritual Arrogance

I wish spiritual arrogance were a minor issue, but I am afraid it is not. For many pastors, it is a principal obstacle to their being open to receiving personal intercession.

I learned about spiritual arrogance from Paul Walker, who at the time was pastoring Mount Paran Church of God in Atlanta, Georgia. I had known Paul for years and greatly admired him. Not only is he a minister in the classical Pentecostal tradition, but he also holds a Ph.D. degree in counseling. When I was working with him, his church was one of the most attended churches in the nation.

Paul told me about a problem that had arisen with a prominent leader in his congregation. Paul had felt that God was directing him to purchase a second campus for his church, namely a large Baptist church building with a modern sanctuary seating approximately 3,000. The Baptist church had been closed for eight years. The purchase of the property, the refurbishing and the necessary additions could all be accomplished with an investment of $10 million, and using the two campuses simultaneously would open the overcrowded Mount Paran to a new phase of growth. But this influential church leader had wanted nothing of it.

Unfortunately the situation escalated until it became critical. The leader's sphere of influence had produced an atmosphere of negativism. The whole church could have been affected to the point of creating a division. It was all the more difficult because Paul and the church leader had been close friends for 25 years. Paul said to me, "I guess all it takes is a difference of opinion to put a long-term friendship on the skids!"

The good news is that Paul had been developing a personal relationship with about 50 intercessors in his church. Among other things, these people were in regular communication with him. It is a well-known fact that trying to get a telephone call through to a megachurch pastor is only slightly less difficult than getting one through to the president at the White House. But Paul had wisely given instructions to his office staff that the 50 intercessors were among those who were to be put through directly to the pastor. In this respect, they had privileges that only administrative and ministry elders shared. Paul affirmed, "I value both their prayer concern and the insights I receive from them."

Paul and the disgruntled church leader had scheduled a meeting that seemed to be a close equivalent to a classic Wild West showdown at high noon. The tension was acute, and the harmony of the church was at stake. However, just before the meeting, one of the intercessors called Paul.

"God has been speaking to me, pastor," she said. "Do you have an important meeting coming up soon?" She, of course, had no information in the natural about what was going on in the high levels of church administration, but God had told her in the Spirit about the meeting.

When Paul affirmed that such a meeting was indeed coming up, this intercessor told him that she thought God was telling her what he should say in the meeting and which Scripture verses he was to use. God instantly gave Paul a deep sense of agreement and confirmation. He took notes and followed the intercessor's advice—and it worked marvelously.

The meeting turned out to be peaceful and harmonious. The church leader and those under his influence received the vision for expansion, and a new dimension of church outreach was achieved. Mount Paran used the new church campus for years, and since that time has added a third campus and a fourth!

Paul and I discussed the fact that many churches split because senior pastors are not sensitive to God's revelation through spiritually mature persons in the congregation. Some would probably have thought, *Why would God give information like this to a little old grandmother in tennis shoes who lives in a two-bit apartment? Why wouldn't God give that kind of information directly to me? After all, I'm the spiritual leader of this church! I'm the one who hears from God where our church is going! Who does she think she is to tell me how to run my church?*

Unfortunately this arrogant attitude is more widespread than we might wish. But I believe that God is raising up high-profile leaders such as Paul Walker to be role models for the rest of us—leaders who have no apologies to make about their maturity, their educational attainments, their spiritual depth and discernment, their leadership skills, the growth and vitality of their churches, or the spiritual levels and contributions of their congregations.

These outstanding leaders have gained prominence, but they are humble enough to know they are not spiritually self-sufficient. They understand the power of intercession as well as Joshua did in the battle of Rephidim. Whether their intercessors have the stature of a Moses or are grandmothers in tennis shoes, such leaders are ready to hear the voice of God and receive the additional spiritual power they need through these precious individuals.

Through intercessors, as prominent a leader as Dwight L. Moody narrowly avoided the trap of spiritual arrogance and blossomed into the influential giant of the faith as we now know him. Moody was already a popular preacher. Even Abraham Lincoln had made a point of visiting Moody's Sunday School in Chicago. But something was lacking, namely a yielding to the full power of the Holy Spirit. I am indebted to Mark Bubeck, who tells the following story in his excellent book *Overcoming the Adversary*.[11]

After one of Moody's meetings, two ladies approached him and said, "Mr. Moody, we have been praying for you." Reflecting some apparent spiritual arrogance, Moody replied rather abruptly, "Why don't you pray for the people?"

The ladies said quietly, "Because you need the power of the Holy Spirit."

Somewhat taken aback, Moody could only respond, "*I* need the power?" The thought was rather preposterous to a spiritual leader who had been visited by none less than the president of the United States.

But the women had heard the Lord well. They customarily sat in the front row of Moody's meetings, deep in prayer as he preached. At first he was annoyed, but gradually God softened his heart. He began to encourage not only their prayers, but also the formation of prayer groups to beseech God that he would be endued with power. Then one day, in New York City, Moody had such an experience of being filled with the Holy Spirit that he admitted he was never able to describe it in words.

One of his biographers says, "God seems to have answered in a mighty way the prayers of these two women, for at this time his life changed considerably from that of a young, somewhat cocky and proud preacher, to a humble, soft and mellow-hearted preacher."[12]

When Moody's spiritual arrogance subsided, the power of God through faithful personal intercessors was released in his life and ministry.

5. Misguided Humility

Humility, of course, is the opposite of arrogance, yet there is some danger that misguided humility can get in the way of receiving intercession. I must admit that I have had some problems with this myself.

The thinking goes like this: *I am no better than anyone else in the Body of Christ. We are all sinners saved by grace. God loves all of His children equally. He does not love me more than the others. Why, then, should*

I expect to receive this powerful intercession *when many of my church members do not have the same privilege? Instead of building a special team of* prayer *partners for myself, might it not be more equitable just to encourage all church members to pray for one another?*

This does not reflect true biblical humility because it fails to recognize that pastors and other leaders are, because of their God-given office, *not* equal to every other member of the Body of Christ. I attempted to explain this matter in some detail in chapter 3, "Why Pastors Need Intercession," so I will not repeat it here. Pastors need intercessory prayer more than every other member of the congregation, and God's plan is to provide it for them. The same applies to apostles, ministers in the workplace, and other Christian leaders.

The part I struggled with was a subsequent question: *Why should I ask someone to give me maybe an hour a day in* prayer, *when I give them back a few seconds or a couple of minutes? It doesn't seem fair.*

I now understand that this is also misguided humility. To counter this, I have learned how to become comfortable with God's design. My intercessors pray for me much more than I pray for them, and they expect nothing different. They are using a spiritual gift of intercession that I do not have. God does certain things through me and my spiritual gifts that He is not doing through my intercessors. The reverse is also true. He does things through them that He does not do through me. We are a team and we need each other! This attitude, I believe, reflects true humility.

In conclusion, I feel that a full appreciation of the operation of the Body of Christ, with all its different members, is a vital key to ridding ourselves of the obstacles that are in the way of receiving personal intercession.

Intercessors may often not be very visible, but they are like the glands in our body that, 24 hours a day, secrete the hormones we need for life, health and energy. Once we understand this, ignorance, rugged individualism, fear, spiritual arrogance and misguided humility will maintain no further foothold in our beings. We will be open to the full ministry of the Holy Spirit and His gifts through the Body of Christ so we can be all that God wants us to be!

Reflection Questions

1. Discuss the difference between *saying* the Lord's Prayer and *praying* the Lord's Prayer. What are the six evident divisions of the Lord's Prayer, and what prayer points might each section include?
2. The phrase "I'll be praying for you!" can mean a great deal or it can mean very little. What would be some concrete examples of each?
3. Do you think that this chapter is too critical of Jimmy Swaggart? Talk about how the issues raised relate to some of his personal problems.
4. Review the story of Paul Walker and his willingness to receive input from his intercessors. Why do you think that many other pastors would not be able to do this?
5. If a Christian leader resists receiving intercession for one or more of the reasons given, what do you think could be done to change this?

THREE TYPES OF PERSONAL INTERCESSORS

Pastors and other Christian leaders who are open to receiving personal intercession and begin asking God for it should soon find that intercession makes a measureable difference in their ministries. I fully recognize that there are some benefits of intercession that defy human measurement, and sometimes these can be among the most important. But those benefits that do happen to be tangible will greatly raise both our faith and our spirits.

God provides intercession in a variety of forms. Most of this chapter will deal with three kinds of personal intercessors. These are individuals who, more than others, are committed to praying on a regular basis for a certain leader.

D. L. Moody's Bedridden Intercessor

Remember how in the last chapter I told of two intercessors whom God used to open Dwight L. Moody to personal intercession in general? Moody was later involved in a more specific incident that shows how God can and does touch an intercessor particularly for a certain event. At times, God will assign what I have called a "crisis intercessor" (rather than simply a "personal intercessor") to a given task.

This happened when Moody was visiting England in 1872 on a kind of sabbatical while his new church was being built in Chicago. His main purpose was to listen to and learn from as many of England's great preachers as possible. But one Sunday he agreed to break his routine and minister in a church in London.

The Sunday morning service turned out to be a disappointing experience. Moody confessed afterward that he had never had such a hard time delivering a sermon in his life. Everything in him and around him seemed perfectly dead. Then the horrible thought came to him that he had to preach there again that night! He went through with it only because he had given his word that he would do so.

But what a difference! That evening the church was packed out, and there was a new and vital spiritual atmosphere. Moody said, "The powers of an unseen world seemed to have fallen upon the audience."[1] Although he had not premeditated it, he decided on the spur of the moment to give an invitation for people to accept Jesus Christ as their personal Savior—and he was astounded when 500 people stood up. He repeated the invitation twice more in an attempt to filter out those who were insincere, but all 500 walked up front to the vestry to pray to receive Christ. A major ongoing revival started in that church and that neighborhood of London that night!

What did intercession have to do with it?

A woman who had attended the morning service had returned home and told her invalid sister that a certain Mr. Moody from the United Sates had preached. The bedridden sister turned pale.

"What," she said, "Mr. Moody from Chicago! I read about him some time ago in an American paper, and I have been praying God to send him to London, and to our church. If I had known he was going to preach this morning I would have eaten no breakfast. I would have spent the whole time in prayer. Now sister, go out of the room, lock the door, send me no dinner; no matter who comes, don't let them see me. I am going to spend the whole afternoon and evening in prayer!"[2]

This story is told by E. M. Bounds, who then comments, "So while Mr. Moody stood in the pulpit that had been like an ice-chamber in the morning, the bedridden saint was holding him up before God, and God, who ever delights to answer prayer, poured out His Spirit in mighty power."[3]

It's hard to doubt that this was a measureable result of focused intercessory prayer!

Gary Greenwald's Team

God frequently empowers ministry through not just one, but a team of intercessors. For example, Gary Greenwald, pastor of Eagle's Nest Church in Irvine, California, had been conducting annual evangelistic crusades in Hawaii. After several years, attendance had grown to 2,000. As his team prayed about it one year, they decided to step out in faith and rent the Hilton Hawaiian ballroom, which seats 4,000. The rental would cost thousands of dollars, and consequently they would need large crowds to pay their bills.

This was such a risky proposition that they sent a team of intercessors from their church in California to stay in the Hilton Hawaiian one week before the crusade for fasting and prayer. The spiritual warfare was intense that week. In fact, the leader of the team suffered so much anxiety during the nights that he almost capitulated and returned home. Several other members of the team were afflicted with sicknesses of one kind or another. But they persisted and felt that they were winning the battle. Their big question was, would they ever fill the ballroom?

The first three nights of the crusade drew 3,000 people, and the final two nights saw the ballroom packed out with 4,000—twice what they had ever had before. It was one of the most powerful crusades they had ever experienced. Many conversions and healing miracles took place, including a severed Achilles tendon being completely restored. The spiritual warfare had been done, and the crusade enjoyed open heavens.

They went ahead and rented the ballroom again the following year. However, because the budget for sending the intercessory team had been so high, they decided to forego it this time. Hawaii usually has an open atmosphere for preaching, but that year guess what? The crusade turned out to be a disaster! The peak attendance was only 1,800. Divisions sprang up among the leadership. Serious issues occurred with the worship leaders. It was a financial wipeout!

It goes without saying that Gary Greenwald learned some lessons about the value of teams of intercessors the hard way that year.

Personal Intercessors

God uses *crisis* intercessors, as we saw with D. L. Moody, and *teams* of intercessors, as with Gary Greenwald. He also uses individual *personal* intercessors: those who make a commitment to pray over an extended period of time for a particular pastor or other Christian leader.

As I have studied the phenomenon of personal intercession for many years in the role of a participant observer, I have found it useful to separate personal intercessors into three approximate categories, which I like to depict as concentric circles around the leader (see graphic).

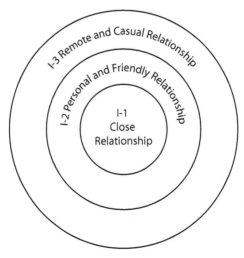

- The inner circle: Here we picture the pastor or other leader, along with what I call "I-1 intercessors."
- The middle circle: This contains the "I-2 intercessors."
- The outer circle: This contains the "I-3 intercessors."

Let's think of the I-1 intercessors as having a *close* relationship with the pastor or leader, the I-2 intercessors as having a *personal and friendly* relationship, and the I-3 intercessors as having a *remote and casual* relationship. I will now describe these types of intercessors in more detail, starting from the outside and working my way in.

I-3 Intercessors

I-3 intercessors can be quite distant from the pastor or leader for whom they pray. Most I-3 intercession is a casual one-way relationship. The leader often may not even know who a certain I-3 intercessor is or that he or she is praying for them and their ministry. I think of Billy Graham, for example. Who knows how many intercessors have prayed faithfully for Billy Graham and his ministry for years, without ever having so much as seen the evangelist in person? However, Billy Graham will be the first to affirm that such intercessors have made all the difference in the world in the effectiveness of his evangelistic ministry.

Of course, leaders generally need a certain amount of visibility beyond the local parish in order to attract these kinds of intercessors. Campus Crusade's founder, Bill Bright, once said, "I would assume that there are hundreds, if not thousands, who pray for me daily from grade school through senior citizens." Bright acknowledges, "If it were not for such intercessors, I am sure I would have been dead long ago from physical exhaustion and would have been totally incapable of doing all that God has enabled me to do."[4]

My friend, the late Omar Cabrera, whose Vision of the Future Church of more than 100,000 in Argentina was one of the world's largest, had a unique system for recruiting I-3 intercessors. He simply asked his church members and their families to pray for him and his wife, Marfa, every time they said grace at meals. An informal calculation estimated that they probably were receiving 20,000 prayers a day through this appeal!

My wife, Doris, and I have a fluctuating list of I-3 intercessors whose names and addresses we know. Some of them have international reputations of their own. Some of them we know only by name; we have never met them personally. There are undoubtedly also many who are praying for us who are not yet on our list. Others are old-time friends or former students. Many of them have the spiritual gift of intercession, but some do not. Some pray primarily for us. Others have included us on a long list of leaders for whom they pray daily.

A memorable experience occurred one day when I was standing in the crowded lobby of the Osaka Hilton Hotel in Japan. A perfect stranger, a Caucasian, walked up to me and asked, "Are you Peter Wagner?" When I told him that I was, he shared that he had prayed for me every morning for the past six years, and he was pleased to finally meet me in person. I was deeply touched by his sincerity. I thanked him, took down his name and address, and wrote him a letter when I got home. I never received a reply. I have no idea where this I-3 intercessor came from or where he went. He seemed to me like a modern Melchizedek!

When I first wrote this book, my favorite I-3 intercessor was then-two-and-a-half-year-old Jess Rainer. This boy's father, Southern Baptist Executive Thom Rainer, whom I mentioned earlier, was at the time doing a Ph.D. at Southern Baptist Theological Seminary on the subject of C. Peter Wagner's theology of church growth. Needless to say, we were keeping in close personal touch during the process. In the midst of it, Thom wrote me a letter discussing an academic matter or two. Then he added a paragraph that said, "By the way, my youngest son (two-and-a-half-year-old Jess) has heard your name so much that he concludes all of his prayers as follows: '. . . and thank you, God, for Peter Wagner, in

Jesus' name, Amen.'" Years later, in a chapter on prayer in one of his subsequent books, Thom brought up the prayer life of his three sons and said of his youngest son, "And Jess, now eleven, has been praying for C. Peter Wagner almost since he learned to talk!"[5] May Jess Rainer's numbers multiply!

I-2 Intercessors

Unlike most I-3 intercessors, typical I-2 intercessors will have a friendly acquaintance and more-or-less regular personal contact with the pastor or leader for whom they pray. Pastors' I-2 intercessors will ordinarily see them in the pulpit every Sunday and shake hands when they exit the church door after the service. They may also cross paths from time to time at other church-related events. But for many, this may be the extent of the personal contact.

One of the things I would like to suggest in this book is that pastors and other leaders take whatever pains might be necessary to cultivate contacts with I-2 intercessors. Most pastors I know experience from time to time that a certain person in the line of those leaving the church service will give them an especially warm handshake and say, "Pastor, I pray for you every day!" I know that we often take this as a polite formality and do not pay any more attention to it than we do to the common statement "I enjoyed the sermon." But in many cases, there might be more to it than simply a formality. At the least it could be opening a pathway worth following, because it might lead to a personal intercessor truly anointed by God to support us in prayer.

A well-developed team of I-2 intercessors enjoys two-way contact with the pastor. It is therefore essential to know who the I-2 intercessors are. Later on I will discuss the ways and means of identifying, screening, recruiting, serving and maintaining these prayer partners. They obviously need to be kept better informed than the I-3 intercessors. They also should make themselves available to be called upon for special prayer if and when a necessity arises.

The optimum size of a group of I-2 intercessors is not yet known, mainly because we do not have a large enough number of viable examples to examine. John Maxwell keeps his group at no more than 100. He has a waiting list of those who would like to be enrolled as prayer partners, and he lets the new ones in only as openings occur. I do think there is an upper limit to I-2 intercessors, though I would not apply a limit to I-3s.

The main principle, as I see it, is to maintain a reasonably high level of commitment among I-2 intercessors. That will come through a certain amount of intentional personal contact, as I will detail later on. Therefore the number of I-2 intercessors should not become too large to sustain necessary contact. It will take time. We'll need to make room in our schedules for intentional contact. How much time is reasonable and appropriate will need to be decided on a case-by-case basis.

My wife, Doris, and I have 18 I-2 intercessors on our prayer team. We live in Colorado Springs; only three of our I-2 intercessors live near us. Others live in California, Florida, Texas, New Mexico and Wyoming. Predictably, 15 of the 18 are women. That's right around the 80 percent female proportion that I mentioned earlier.

The Gift of Intercession

Not all of our personal intercessors have the spiritual gift of intercession, though most of them do. We do not regard those who don't have the gift as second-class citizens. Some who do not have the gift are actually more committed to supporting us day in and day out than some who do. On a football team, the guards (whose names you hardly ever hear) are no less important than the running backs. It takes the whole group working together as a team to win.

When we began the process of building a team of I-1 and I-2 intercessors, we were among the pioneers. We had few established patterns from the past to guide us. Fortunately we were in a position where we could talk amongst ourselves and support one another.

For example, one of our original I-2 intercessors, Pam Marhad, had to work through her role as one of those who did not have the spiritual gift of intercession. She wrote about her experience in *Body Life*, our Sunday School class monthly newsletter. In her article, Pam said, "More often than not, when I decide I will pray for certain people or situations, a feeling of frustration and 'what's the use?' overcomes my good intentions and defeats me."

As she prayed about it, Pam felt that the Lord took her to the parable of the talents in Matthew 25. In this passage, it is clear that God is the One who decides who gets what talents and how many. Seeing that, Pam confessed, "I've been guilty of looking around and saying in my heart, 'Lord, I'm just a one-talent pray-er. Others you have made five-talent pray-ers—let them pray. My prayers probably don't matter.'"

Once she realized the error of her ways, Pam wisely concluded that all God expected of her was to use the resources He had entrusted to her—nothing more, nothing less. "As I'm faithful and obedient to use what He's given," she said, "then He's free to give me more if He chooses. If I don't value His gifts to me and neglect them because they don't measure up to what I see others doing, then I tie the Lord's hands in my life and find myself on the outside looking in with envy and resentment."[6] It could not be said better.

How Long?

When we invite I-2 intercessors to be part of our prayer-partners team, Doris and I expect that the relationship will continue indefinitely. At the same time, however, we recognize that God may assign certain intercessors to us for a season, and then give them other assignments. During the first few years after we formed our team of prayer partners in 1988, several dropped off and several were added. However, in later years the turnover has gone down to nearly zero. The only attrition we have seen recently has been the death of an intercessor.

Doris and I are the only leaders for whom some of our I-2 intercessors pray regularly, but others pray for several leaders. Barbara Byerly is a good example. When she first committed to pray for us, she told us that she also prayed for Jane Hansen, Joy Dawson, Cindy Jacobs and Mary Lance Sisk. Part of Barbara's highly developed ministry of personal intercession has been a keen sensitivity to the "dancing Spirit of God" over those for whom she prays. For a season, she may find God burdening her more for one than for the others. Then the priorities may change again.

Back when I was first writing this book (and probably *because* I was writing it), I remember receiving a note from Barbara that said, "Peter, you are coming up No. 1 in my prayer discharge right now. It's nothing I've done or failed to do. Nothing you've done. I would guess that God is orchestrating a new realm of prayer support at this time." I was deeply grateful for this, because *Prayer Shield* has subsequently turned out to be a great blessing to many through the years.

Feeling the Wind of the Spirit

Back when Doris and I were leading the AD2000 United Prayer Track, we happened to be making a trip to England to do a pastors' seminar. Just before we left, one of our I-2 intercessors, Dave Rumph (who at the time was a research engineer at our local Xerox branch), told us that he sensed the Lord was arranging something special for us in England with Roger Forster. I had heard about Roger but had never met him personally. My assigned ministry in England had nothing directly to do with Roger or with the Icthus movement he was leading.

Then, also before we left, Barbara Byerly phoned with a prophetic word she had received for us. I asked her to write it out for me. In part it said, "Feel the wind of My Spirit. I am lifting you higher and higher. You need no effort on your part for My wind will lift you. Greater days are ahead. Far more than you can yet see are My plans for you!"

Sure enough, the trip to England unexpectedly became a crucial milestone in our ministry. Not so much because of my scheduled pastors' seminar, but because of an unplanned meeting with none other than Roger Forster and Gerald Coates, two of the leaders of the newly born March for Jesus movement. In that meeting, God began to give direction to Doris and me to take leadership of what we came to call "A Day to Change the World," which would be held on June 25, 1994, in connection with our United Prayer Track. The plans for this day soon became "far more than we could see" (as Barbara's prophecy indicated) before we went to England. It turned out to be the largest international prayer meeting recorded up to that time!

Why do I bring this up? Here were two I-2 intercessors who were so tuned in to our ministry and God's plans for us that God used them and their prayers (as well as the prayers of others from whom we had not heard) to move us into an unanticipated, exciting and awesome new area of service for God's kingdom.

Before I move on to discussing the innermost circle, allow me to share one additional story about how God uses I-2 intercessors to support ministry. While at Fuller Seminary, I did most of my teaching in one-week or two-week modules. During the one-week sessions, I taught mornings and afternoons each day. It was a concentrated schedule, but teaching usually increases my energy level rather than diminishing it. On a certain occasion, however, I was bothered that one of my weeklong church growth courses was not going well. On the Saturday before the class started, I began feeling washed out. Sunday was more of the same. When I began teaching on Monday, I had virtually no energy, and I felt as though I was carrying a heavy load on my shoulders. Tuesday was almost as bad. I was just going through the motions. But on Wednesday, the load completely lifted. I could relax while I taught, and I could think clearly and creatively for the first time since Saturday.

Soon afterward, no fewer than three of our I-2 intercessors approached me, one at a time, and asked, "What happened last Wednesday? Why did I feel you needed special prayer that day?" When I told them what had happened, we rejoiced that God had yoked us together in ministry and that the answers to their prayers had been so tangible.

I-1 Intercessors

God calls I-1 intercessors to have a special, close relationship with the pastor or other leader. Sometimes this involves a close social relationship; sometimes it is a largely spiritual or professional relationship. All of the I-1 intercessors I know have the spiritual gift of intercession. Through it they have developed an intimacy with the Father that allows them to hear His voice and know His purposes more clearly than most.

Leaders I know who relate to I-1 prayer partners sometimes have three of them, sometimes two, but most frequently one. Through the years, God has assigned three of these intercessors to Doris and me, one at a time. The first was a member of our Sunday School class, Cathy Schaller. The second was Alice Smith of the U.S. Prayer Center in Houston, Texas. After some years, Alice asked to move from I-1 to I-2; fortunately, God had already prepared Chuck Pierce to take her place. We mutually expect to continue in this relationship for the foreseeable future.

The Ladder and the Fall

The memorable day on which we began our I-1 relationship with Cathy Schaller was March 25, 1983. Why do we remember the date so specifically? That evening at 8:30, I went out to our garage in Altadena, California, to get some income tax papers. I had stored them up on a loft in the garage—10 feet off the cement floor. As I had been doing repeatedly for years, I climbed the stepladder to get onto the loft. My head was 12 feet above the floor when I began moving from the ladder to the loft.

Then, in an instant, something pulled that ladder out from under me (I have chosen those words carefully!), and I took a free fall, landing on the back of my head, my neck, and my upper back. During the second or so it took to complete the 12-foot drop, I was thinking to myself, *This is it!* but I was able to shout loudly enough so that Doris came running to the garage. My next-door neighbor, Randy Becker, also heard the commotion and rushed over. He and Doris called 911 and prayed.

The paramedics came and took me in an ambulance to the emergency room at St. Luke's Hospital. They put me through all the required tests and X-rays, and a couple of hours later sent me home. Remarkably, they had found no structural damage or internal injuries. Yes, I was badly bruised, stiff and sore for several weeks, but I suffered no after-effects at all from what was the most serious accident of my life.

Meanwhile, that evening, Cathy and her husband, Mike, had taken a group of young girls to a Ken Medema concert at a church about 10 miles from my home. Some months previously, Cathy and Mike had joined Lake Avenue Church, and they had begun attending our 120 Fellowship Sunday School class. However, we had not come to really know one another yet.

A Life and Death Battle

When she and her husband returned to their seats after an intermission, Cathy happened to notice that her watch said 8:30. They had begun to dim the house lights for effect when an incredibly powerful cloud of darkness seemed to envelop Cathy. The presence of evil was so strong around her that she could actually smell it. In her spirit, she accurately identified it as a spirit of death and destruction. The Holy Spirit spoke to her, saying, "It has come to destroy someone you have a relationship to, but not one of your children." She then felt a shield of protection raised between her and the force of evil, so she knew she was personally safe.

All this happened in an instant, and without hesitation, Cathy began to pray under her breath for "legions of angels." Then a severe pain came into her back, and it felt as though her back was breaking. As she squirmed with pain, Mike whispered, "What's wrong?"

All Cathy could say was, "My spirit is troubled and my back hurts." Mike laid on hands and prayed that her back would be healed. Cathy continued to pray in the Spirit for 20 minutes, and then she sensed a total release. The battle was over; the evil cloud left; she relaxed, enjoyed the rest of the concert, and went home to bed.

Late that night, Cathy's bedside telephone rang. It was our Sunday School class president alerting the class prayer chain to pray for me because I had suffered a terrible accident. Cathy instantly knew in her spirit that this was what she had been praying for at the concert, but the president could not confirm the exact time of my fall.

Cathy's call to Doris and me the next morning was one of the most incredible telephone calls I can remember. We could not prove it in a court of law, but Doris and I do not need a court of law to be convinced that Cathy's faithfulness in prayer that night literally saved my physical life. Satan had sent an evil spirit (which we later actually identified and located, but that is another story) to kill me. For years after that, Doris and I took Cathy and Mike out to dinner every March 25 to celebrate my deliverance from "The Fall" and express our gratitude to her for ministering to us.

Seven Years of Learning

"The Fall" was the dramatic beginning of a prayer partner relationship of seven years, which ultimately changed the direction of our lives and ministry. At the beginning of that season, none of us knew much about prayer or personal intercession.

Cathy later recalled that some time before the incident, someone had casually mentioned to her that she might have the gift of intercession. Subsequently she had received strong internal impressions about relatives who were in danger on two separate occasions, but she had no idea what to do with such impressions. Unfortunately, both of her relatives died! You can imagine how grateful I am that the third time she received an impression, she did respond. When she called me the next morning, I said, "Cathy, do you realize that this is a gift of intercession?"

Over the next several years, Cathy related to Doris and me as our first I-1 intercessor. Those were the years when the seed thoughts for this book were first planted. Cathy was learning what it meant to be a personal intercessor. We were learning how to receive intercession. It was a season during which we went through our share of ups and downs. But, looking back, we know that we needed both the ups and the downs to learn what we know now.

After seven years, Cathy's gift had developed to the extent that God released her from her assignment to us and reassigned her to be the full-time prayer leader for an international mission agency.

Intercessors Need Help, Too

One of the things we learned about I-1 intercessors is that they, particularly during critical times, need intercessory help themselves. The spiritual warfare they find themselves engaged in on behalf of the pastor or leader can become overwhelming. Moses, you may recall, needed the help of Aaron and Hur in order to intercede effectively for Joshua during the battle of Rephidim. Along these lines, I recall one time when Cathy desperately needed some Aarons and Hurs.

What happened?

During the 1980s, I had invited John Wimber to help me teach a new course on Signs, Wonders and Church Growth at Fuller Seminary. The course stirred up a very intense controversy, and I was at the center of unrest for years. This was by far the most painful trial I had personally endured since leaving the mission field in Bolivia. And it lasted for three and a half years!

Without going into details here, suffice it to say that after three and a half years, I had come to the end of my patience. I had been on the defensive for all that time, and I was getting prepared to switch to offense. A crucial showdown meeting had been scheduled with the seminary Faculty Senate. My temper was on edge and my guns, so to speak, were loaded for the shootout.

I showed up at the meeting. A grim-faced theology dean entered and displayed a copy of my book *How to Have a Healing Ministry* on the table in front of him. A distinguished professor of theology brought another copy and put it on the table as well. I knew that both of them had IQs much higher than mine, and I became very apprehensive about the impending arguments. I thought I was in for it!

But, incredibly, the meeting was called to order and there was no showdown! The proposal I presented was somehow passed unanimously! No one was nasty. A couple of rather routine questions were addressed to me, but nothing else. I had my guns loaded, but I did not have to pull the trigger. Why? I have no doubt that the spiritual warfare behind this whole scenario had been completed before the meeting began. And I believe that Cathy, as my I-1 intercessor, was the principal agent for winning that spiritual battle.

It was not easy for her by any means. Looking back, I am convinced that this Faculty Senate meeting was a significant milestone in my personal ministry career, if not also for the Fuller Seminary community in general. Because of that, the warfare, not surprisingly, was far more intense than usual.

What was going on behind the scenes?

During the week leading up to the Faculty Senate meeting:

- Cathy's car was totaled and she received a serious whiplash. The other driver was clearly at fault, but decided to sue Cathy!

- The family of a student in the Christian junior high school where Cathy was then teaching had produced a written list of 30 trumped-up charges against both her competence and her character. She was emotionally devastated! The charges were being taken to her school board, which coincidentally was meeting to consider them on the very day of the Faculty Senate meeting.
- Cathy's kitchen caught on fire, and the fire burned a hole through her kitchen floor!

Aarons and Hurs

More than ever before, Cathy needed her Aarons and Hurs. Whereas God only sent two of these supporters to Moses, He sent nine to Cathy!

The first one we found out about was Dave Rumph, one of our I-2 intercessors. Dave did not have the gift of intercession, but he did have the gift of encouragement. God assigned Dave to pray for Cathy at that time, and also to call her on the telephone several times during the week.

After the fact, we learned about eight others who had been praying for Cathy. Christy Graham, whom I have previously mentioned as an example of a crisis intercessor, had been assigned by God to pray intensely for Cathy six weeks before the Faculty Senate meeting, and she had been praying faithfully every day.

Lil Walker, who is now one of our I-2 intercessors but at that time was not, was assigned to pray for Cathy. Linda Stanberry, a furloughed missionary taking my courses at Fuller, received a week-long burden to pray for Cathy. Nanette Brown, a member of our Sunday School class, was awakened at 3:30 A.M. the morning of Cathy's school board meeting, and she prayed for Cathy for three-quarters of an hour before going back to sleep. There were four others as well.

Meanwhile, Cathy was doing for me what Euodia and Syntyche had done for the apostle Paul, namely "spiritual warfare on my behalf." I did not have to go through the potentially explosive Faculty Senate debate I had anticipated. Cathy had taken the brunt of the spiritual attack potentially aimed at me. It never occurred to her to complain. She was using her spiritual gift and flowing with the Holy Spirit, and her prayers for me were being answered. But she needed help. None of the nine people who helped her was praying for me at the time. Satan was trying to get Cathy's arms down (to use the analogy of Moses praying for Joshua), but God provided her with nine Aarons and Hurs to hold up her arms until the battle was finished.

The results of their prayers? The lawsuit connected to the accident was dropped; the school board dismissed the charges totally; and the fire insurance paid for rebuilding Cathy's kitchen floor much better than it had been before the fire. Cathy told us that the week following the Faculty Senate meeting was one of the most relaxed, pleasant and unstressful weeks she could remember, both in her school and with her family. The battle had been fought and won!

Quenching the Fiery Darts!

A very helpful analysis of the role of personal intercessors comes from Sylvia Evans of Elim Bible Fellowship in Lima, New York. She says that one of God's most wonderful blessings is His faithfulness "to waken intercessors for the night watch or an early morning watch and to place them on duty to head off the enemy." She sees intercessors as watchers constantly on the alert to be assigned their position in battle.

In discussing the full armor of God as described in Ephesians 6, Evans interprets the passage as suggesting that the intercessor "is to be able to aggressively withstand the enemy, taking the attack for others who may be the real target. The watchman must be able to quench all the fiery darts, not only against himself or herself, but also against the ones for whom they are standing watch."[7]

Doris and I are thankful to God for raising up intercessors who have been willing and able to take the fiery darts of the enemy for us. Other than our immediate family, they are the most precious group of people related to our lives and our ministry. We rejoice that we are now seeing God spreading this kind of spiritual power throughout the Body of Christ.

Reflection Questions

1. This chapter gives illustrations of how prayer affected the ministries of D. L. Moody and Gary Greenwald. Could you give an example of how a similar thing happened for a leader you know of?
2. Mention some people you know who serve as I-3 intercessors for pastors or other leaders, and talk about that relationship.
3. Pam Marhad's experience is helpful to many Christians who desire to serve God with all their hearts. Why do you think that so many can identify with her?
4. What do you think happened in the heavenlies when Cathy Schaller prayed for me during my fall from the ladder?
5. As this chapter shows, serious intercession for a pastor or other leader can open one to severe attacks of the enemy. Some question whether it is worth the risk. What do you think?

RECRUITING PRAYER PARTNERS

I believe this will turn out to be the most vital chapter of this book for many of the pastors and other Christian leaders who desire to see the power of personal intercession begin to flow through their lives and ministries. Satan is not ignorant of the threat that intercession for pastors poses to his evil plans. He wants to mess up pastors and neutralize their spiritual influence in their churches and communities to the highest degree possible. Intercessors, particularly of the kind I have been describing, set back the enemy's work in a decisive way whenever they go into action.

A tactic that the devil has all-too-skillfully employed in the past is to manipulate pastors into making poor choices of prayer partners. This can and does short-circuit receiving personal intercession in two ways.

The first device the enemy uses to discourage intercession is to cause pastors or other leaders to choose wrong intercessors who unfortunately can end up doing them more harm than good. This would be bad enough in itself, but it also can lead to the second tactic. One bad experience can cause a pastor not only to give up on the concept of personal intercession altogether, but also to move on from there and begin to persuade others that it is unwise. One prominent leader I know rejected personal intercession for himself for years. During that time, he was teaching many of his followers to avoid intercessors as well—until God sovereignly brought him into close relationship with an experienced intercessor who displayed high integrity and who eventually caused him to change his mind.

Results of a Poor Choice

When I was teaching personal intercession in my Fuller Doctor of Ministry courses, many of my students became motivated to seek personal intercession for themselves. When these pastors returned to their churches, some had functioning teams of prayer partners activated within weeks, in a few cases within days, where God had obviously already been preparing the way for them. They just needed to know that it was OK. The overwhelming majority of reports I received were positive and enthusiastic. But not all. One of the pastors, who had an especially analytical mind, not only had a bad experience, but also turned that experience into a term paper for my advanced seminar.

This pastor from the Midwest wrote under the pen name of Paul A. Freedman. Fortunately, he had enough personal stability and a high enough level of self-esteem not to be devastated by his negative experience. He was able to think positively, learn from his setbacks, and move forward aggressively on the basis of what he had learned. No wonder his church was a growing church. Despite his initial disappointment, he did and still does believe that "intercessory prayer is one of the most important elements of successful ministry today." He affirmed that since hearing of personal prayer partners in my seminar, "I have come to greatly appreciate and rely upon the ministry of I-1 intercessors."

Paul Freedman's story vividly illustrates what can happen when the wrong people move into the position of an I-1 intercessor, and what can change when the right ones are there.

Paul had begun to look for an I-1 intercessor when he returned home after taking my course, but his church happened to be facing another critical situation at the time. He had previously given high priority to leading a strong prayer ministry in his church; however, as the church continued to grow he found he could give less and less of his time to it. This caused deep frustration, and it soon became obvious that the entire prayer ministry needed to be updated and reorganized.

Consequently, Freedman was happy and relieved when "a dearly loved and well-respected member of the church approached me to tell me that she had been praying specifically for me on a daily basis, and that she saw a great need to reorganize the prayer ministry of our church." Paul saw this connection as meeting both needs at once. He invited the woman to become an I-1 intercessor for him and also to take charge of the church's struggling prayer ministry.

From Doubts to Depression

Bad move! He says, "I was expecting relief and new strength, but things just got worse!"

Since the woman was an I-1 intercessor, Paul began to share some of his more personal prayer requests with her. He soon noticed that she seemed to differ with him on certain theological points, but he brushed them aside as minor issues. He later found out, much to his dismay, that these had been *major* concerns in the mind of this woman.

As the arrangement continued, Paul began to notice that his ministry seemed to be less effective. More people than usual were dissatisfied. He needed to expend higher levels of physical and mental energy to get the same results. He was constantly tired. He became angry. The anger led to frustration, and the frustration led to depression. He says, "I was losing my love for the ministry. I knew the Lord was still there for me, but I didn't want to be there for the Lord anymore. I was angry with God and angry with myself. I just wanted out!"

Then the enemy, having Paul Freedman spiritually and psychologically where he wanted him, unloaded the brunt of his attack. During one week, two women, unrelated to each other, came to Paul for "counseling." Remarkably, both of them had developed an infatuation for him, and they let him know that they would be available to him any time he had the desire. Fortunately Paul's internal alarm system went off. He says, "I recognized the spiritual attacks for what they were. I quickly decided to get my wife and get away!"

The couple isolated themselves from the congregation for a month, seeking new objectivity and a renewed relationship with God. The Lord faithfully met them in their need, and He revealed to Paul what the cause of the problems was. Paul suddenly saw clearly that the woman he had selected as an I-1 intercessor and asked to lead the church's prayer ministry was not God's choice. Here is the way he puts it: "She was not submitted to my ministry nor open to my spiritual authority. Rather, she wanted to change me through prayer. She sought to control me by asking God to change me into something that she believed was correct."

Meanwhile the woman's influence had spread. She turned some of the I-2 intercessors against the pastor and caused discontent, disunity, anger, and even rebellion among church members. Several families left the church as a result.

Once he realized all of this, Paul faced what he anticipated could be his biggest challenge of all. How would he tell this woman what he now knew without causing an explosion and a possible church split? By then, she wielded a tremendous amount of influence in the congregation.

The good news is that God had known all about the situation, and He had gone ahead of Paul to change things. Before the Freedmans had returned from their vacation, the woman and her family left the church, citing "theological differences" as the reason!

Replacing the False Intercessor

As it turned out, this incredibly smooth solution to such a thorny disaster happened because of *positive* intercessory prayer. How? Again, before Paul returned from his vacation, God not only removed the former intercessor, but also replaced her with people who eventually became three new I-1 intercessors. None of the three knew either of the other two. But all had been praying fervently and had been keeping journals of what the Lord was revealing to them for Paul. Each of them had been praying for months previously. Undoubtedly, it was the foothold of the enemy through the false intercessor that had prevented the pastor from recognizing the three as intercessors sooner.

When the new intercessors got to know one another and began comparing notes, the consistency and agreement in what God had been showing all three were astounding. Remarkably, two of them, according to their journals, had clearly known months previously that Paul would be tempted by "lustful and foolish" women. In his paper, he rightly concludes that "the intercessors having received advanced warnings to pray for me at that time may well have saved my ministry." Remember that Paul's "internal alarm system" went off after the two seductive women visited him? What made it go off, when we know of too many other cases of pastors whose alarm systems did *not* go off in similar circumstances? Personal intercession!

The upshot of all of this? Within a few months, a new prayer ministry was installed and the church began to grow once again. Paul says, "During a three-month period, under the prayers of God's chosen warriors, our church received into membership the largest number of new members in our history. We also witnessed average weekly offerings hit an all-time high!"

The risk of making a mistake such as Pastor Freedman did comes with the territory. His was not the first, and it will not be the last. But I believe that we can learn from him and from the experiences of others in order to keep such mistakes to a minimum.

Recruiting Short-Term Pray-ers

None of what I have said so far should lead us to imagine that the only effective prayer that pastors and other Christian leaders need to receive is that of recognized I-1, I-2 or I-3 intercessors. For example, many members of my 120 Fellowship Sunday School class did not necessarily pray for me on a daily or other regular basis, but they did pray when there was a special need. I considered it important to let them know of my prayer needs in general, and some more specifically. I made a practice of sharing prayer requests every week.

Sandra Gilbreath, who was one of our I-2 intercessors, also headed the prayer ministry of the 120 Fellowship. Sandra gave leadership to the prayer ministry during class time; she identified and recruited those who had a special desire to pray for the people and the needs of the class; she led a pre-class prayer meeting; she processed prayer request slips filled out in class; and she organized prayer chains for special needs as they came up.

For example, when Doris or I, or both of us, went away on some ministry trips, Sandra would organize a prayer and fasting chain. We did not request it for every trip, wanting to avoid its becoming a formality or routine. But when we felt that a certain ministry might be a special target of spiritual warfare, Sandra activated her prayer chain.

Sandra frequently would cut, paste and photocopy pages from a date book that contained spaces for all the days we would be gone, plus one week after the trip. (We had learned from hard experience that often the most severe spiritual attacks would come right after, not during, a ministry assignment.) Sandra would make an announcement in class, and then pass the prepared sheet around. Class members, whether they were our formal prayer partners or not, would fill in their names on one or more days on which they promised to fast at least one meal and pray for us and our ministry. Sandra then gave us a photocopy of the filled-in calendar, and reminded those who had signed up when their day came around.

How did this work? I happened to save my copy of the prayer schedule for a trip I made to Argentina and Brazil, along with some notes I made on it. Each day had at least two persons praying, and some had as many as four. The most visible attacks on me during that trip were physical. There may, of course, have been other attacks that did not come to my attention because my prayer chain headed them off. But I see in my notes that at one point I lost my voice, once I had a stuffed-up head, once I had a serious cough, and once I suffered an acute attack of diverticulitis. Every one of these afflictions was remarkably short-lived, and none became a barrier to my ministry. I believe the enemy was once again frustrated by the prayers of the saints!

Recruiting I-3 Intercessors

There is ordinarily some overlap between what I have called "short-term pray-ers" and I-3 intercessors. Theoretically there would be no upper limit to the number of I-3 intercessors who could support a given individual or ministry. The one limitation I am aware of is the ability to keep them informed. Later I want to discuss this in some detail, but here I will simply mention that one way to keep I-3 intercessors informed is through a periodic email to them. If the number gets too large, it becomes more and more challenging to maintain up-to-date email addresses.

Doris and I currently have 85 I-3 intercessors to whom we try to send periodic emails. We would like to have more than 85, and I know that there are an unknown number of others who also pray for us regularly. We try to keep the I-3 list to as high a level of commitment and quality as we can. We do not add names easily or haphazardly. Quite frequently, a stranger will come up to me during a conference, introduce himself or herself, and then say, "I pray for you every day!" This does not automatically trigger an invitation to be an I-3 intercessor. I rely strongly on the Lord telling me what to do at that moment.

From time to time, but not always, I sense that God is giving me a green light; in that case I simply say, "Thank you. Would you like us to send you information occasionally?"

If the person replies, "Yes," I offer him or her my business card and suggest that he or she email me and remind me of our conversation. Not everyone follows through; the ones who go to this trouble are probably qualified as I-3 intercessors, so I invite them.

I could do more. I could distribute response devices at my various speaking engagements for people to fill in with their contact information, indicating that they would pray for us regularly. I could send an email blast urging people to sign up. I could make an appeal on Facebook. This could possibly give me a mailing list of 10,000 over a relatively short period of time. But the commitment level would be sure to drop considerably. Many of these would regard our subsequent emails as just another newsletter and delete them without paying any more attention.

Having said all this, let's agree that no prayer is wasted. I would rather have 100 pastors pray for me for a week or two after a pastors' seminar than not have them pray at all. So I keep asking people to pray for us. I recommend that pastors also do this week after week from their pulpits. The more personal the requests, the better—at least to a point. Leaders of ministries should include prayer requests in their newsletters. Many pray-ers will respond positively.

Recruiting I-2 Intercessors

I like the formula that Cindy Jacobs recommends for recruiting I-2 intercessors. She uses Luke 11:9, where we are told to *ask* and it will be given, *seek* and we will find, *knock* and it will be opened to us. *Asking*, according to the Jacobs Formula, is praying for the Lord to touch the potential prayer partners and prepare them. *Seeking* is to sit down and make a list of all those who, from general observation or past experience, seem as though they might be praying for you or willing to pray for you. *Knocking* is then getting in contact with those on the list by email or by telephone.

Cindy says that when she first heard about personal prayer partners, she and her family were going through hard times. Her husband was having unusual problems on the job, the children were experiencing severe harassment, and it seemed that they were barely moving from crisis to crisis. One day Cindy said, "Enough is enough! I have had it with this attack!" So she prayed that the Lord would send personal intercessors. Then she made a list and contacted the people on it, stressing that the prayer requests were to be kept confidential. The letter she wrote, she says, "explained that we would be sharing intimate details that were to be revealed to no one other than our prayer partners."[1]

What were the results? The response was tremendously encouraging. Within a week, all of the immediate problems had cleared up. Cindy says, "The prayer partners for Generals International are all top-notch intercessors, and we are greatly touched by their labor of love on our behalf. Since they have been praying for us, our ministry has exploded in growth."[2]

Asking God

Some leaders who understand personal intercession feel that they should not actively recruit I-2 intercessors, but should stop at the first part of the Jacobs Formula and simply ask God for them. This was the policy of Paul Walker, then pastor of Mount Paran Church of God in Atlanta. As I mentioned in a previous chapter, Paul knew of 50 I-2 intercessors in his congregation who prayed for him. They were mostly mature women. Each of them, so far as he could keep track, was directly and individually called of God to that ministry. Paul told me personally that he once had an I-1 intercessor, and that he would welcome another, but he felt that God should take the initiative, and he was patiently waiting for Him to do so.

One of the most dramatic answers to prayer concerning I-2 intercessors that I have heard occurred in Kenya. One of my students, Francis Kamau, who was an Assemblies of God pastor, said that he had three close personal (I-1) intercessors, but he had never thought much about adding another level to his team of prayer partners. He then took my classes and learned my terminology, which fit his situation exactly.

One day, all three I-1s came to Francis and said that God was telling them he needed some more prayer partners, and that God would give them to him. The four of them agreed to pray for I-2 intercessors for a week. Sure enough, on Friday of that week, Pastor Kamau received no fewer than 22 telephone calls, all from people who said words to the effect: "Pastor, God has told me to pray for you!" I jokingly asked him if he would mind loaning me some of those I-1 prayer partners!

Seeking and Knocking

The second and third parts of the Jacobs Formula, "seek and knock," also work for some. Jerry Johnson, formerly the executive pastor of Lake Avenue Church, became motivated to recruit prayer partners when he first visited South Korea and spent some time with God on one of the prayer mountains there. When he returned, he increased his own daily prayer time to one hour, and he began asking God for I-2 intercessors. He then made a list and wrote to 40 people, challenging them to promise to pray for him at least one day per week, and asking them to indicate on which day or days they would be praying.

Of the 40 people on Jerry's list, 31 responded, and several of them committed to pray for him on more than one day per week. Jerry later reported to me that the number had risen to 53 prayer partners. He knew that on some days, at least 6 or 7 were praying for him. He has personally noticed, and his church members have also noticed, a significant increase in power and effectiveness in his ministry since he first recruited prayer partners.

Doris and I have seen both parts of the Jacobs Formula work. We began by personally recruiting our initial small group of I-2 prayer partners. At that point, Cathy Schaller had served as our I-1 intercessor for five years. In order to learn more about how personal intercession worked, Doris and I took Cathy and her family to San Diego for a weekend to enjoy some R&R and also to research the prayer dynamic at Skyline Wesleyan Church, then under the leadership of John Maxwell. By the time we came home, we were convinced that we needed to take some action.

Forming the Team

At that time Cathy was also the leader of the Sunday School class pastoral care team, and she knew more about the members of the class than anyone else. So I called her and said, "Cathy, would you please make a list of class members who you know are already praying for us on a regular basis, and then approach them one by one to see if they feel led to commit themselves to an I-2 relationship with us? Above all, when you ask them, do it in such a way that they will be able to say no very easily if they do not feel God is calling them to do it."

I felt that this was the wisest procedure, because if I had approached people personally, I suspected that some, just out of courtesy, would not be able to bring themselves to say no, even if they really felt like they should do so. Our approach worked well, and we brought together our initial team of 13 I-2 intercessors, who, along with Cathy, made a prayer partners team of 14.

I do not recall how many said no, but I did make a mental note that one of them was Lil Walker, a class member known to have the spiritual gift of intercession. Lil told Cathy, and then me personally, that although God did direct her to pray for me from time to time, He had assigned her as an I-1 intercessor to our pastor, Paul Cedar, and she did not feel free to take on any other regular commitments.

To complete that story, Paul Cedar eventually left, Lil was released from her assignment to him, and she has been one of our long-term I-2s ever since. My point is that it is very important to allow people the greatest freedom to turn down the invitation if it does not seem right at the time. As a matter of fact, I was on Jerry Johnson's original list of 50, and I turned down his invitation. The last thing either one of us needed was an intercessor like Paul Freedman's!

The Rule: Slow and Cautious

Even when God seemingly initiates the process, Doris and I have been very slow and cautious about inviting additional I-2 intercessors onto our team. A significant turning point in our ministry came at the great Lausanne Congress on World Evangelization held in Manila in the summer of 1989.

At the Lausanne Congress, we sensed that God was putting strategic-level spiritual warfare on our ministry agenda at least for the decade of the 1990s. At that time we did not know of the far-reaching scope of this change, but God obviously did, and He began to provide some world-class intercessors to add to our team of I-2s. Truly, the intensity of the personal spiritual warfare we have been engaged in since then has escalated considerably, and we clearly needed more help than we had previously.

The first additional I-2 intercessor was Cindy Jacobs, whom I have mentioned several times. We had become acquainted with her a few months earlier at a Prayer Summit in Washington, D.C., and Doris and I quickly formed a close personal friendship with Cindy and her husband, Mike. We did several things together, but it still took Doris and me a number of months before we approached Cindy to join our ministry as a prayer partner. She told us that she had known by the Holy Spirit for some time that we were going to invite her, but she had patiently waited.

Cindy then introduced us to our next new I-2 intercessor, Barbara Byerly. We had never heard of Barbara until we met her in Manila, where she was part of the 24-hour on-site intercession team praying for the Lausanne Congress. Cindy privately let us know that Barbara had gained one of the highest international reputations as an intercessor that she was aware of. We liked Barbara and her husband, Jim, very much, but never dreamed that God would give us this woman of whom Cindy had spoken so highly as a personal prayer partner.

However, one day, near the end of the Manila conference, Barbara called us aside and said she wanted to talk to us. She told us she had not slept the night before—not a totally unusual report from an intercessor! But then she added that the reason God had kept her awake the whole night was to give her the assignment to pray for us! She told us there were only two others God had assigned her to pray for at that time, namely Jane Hansen and Joy Dawson.

Coming from a woman who was so widely admired for her ability to hear from God, this was astounding to us. Nevertheless, we, as always, were cautious. And Barbara was very sweet about it; she was never at all pushy, even though she already knew what the final outcome would be. It took us four months to be convinced that the door was truly open. I later told her that it was a special challenge to pray for seminary professors, because they are trained to be overly cautious. Even after we had decided to move forward with the invitation, we hedged a bit by asking Cindy if she would call Barbra and tell her how we felt, giving her plenty of space to say no to our request. She, of course, said yes, and we have had a wonderful relationship ever since. We were even fortunate enough to have Barbara on our Global Harvest Ministries staff for several years.

Recruiting I-1 Intercessors

If it takes more care to recruit I-2 intercessors than I-3s, obviously the greatest care needs to be exercised with I-1 intercessors. At this point I agree with Paul Walker that God Himself must be the one who initiates the contact. I think that the only advisable procedure for us who are leaders is to go directly to God and *ask* Him for these closest prayer partners, starting and stopping with point one of the Jacobs Formula.

I have already related the incredible story of how God used Satan's plot to kill me in my garage to bond us with Cathy Schaller as our first I-1 intercessor. An equally supernatural event brought us together with our next I-1 intercessor, Alice Smith.

Doris and I were in Seoul, South Korea, in the summer of 1990, participating in David Yonggi Cho's annual Church Growth International conference. I am on Cho's board, and at that time I was teaching in his conference almost every year. That year Cho made a mistake that he has not since repeated, namely deciding to hold the plenary teaching session in the Yoido Full Gospel Church sanctuary itself, instead of in one of the smaller chapels as had previously been the custom. The sanctuary seats 25,000; because only 3,000 were in attendance at the conference, the most prominent thing we were looking at from the platform was empty seats!

In fact, I will go so far as to confess that I had a yellow pad in my hands, but instead of taking notes (I had heard the talk before!), I was catching up on some urgent correspondence. I would naturally look up and nod my head in agreement with Cho from time to time, and once when I did this my eyes unmistakably focused on a person sitting so far away that I could tell it was a woman but could not see any features. When my eyes fell on her, God spoke very clearly in my spirit, saying, "She is an intercessor!" I thought that it was nice to have at least one intercessor in the crowd, and I went on writing letters.

However, twice more the exact same thing happened. By then it was remarkable enough for me to make a mental note, but I still was not catching on as I should have been. I had spotted two of my Fuller students in the audience, so at the break I left the platform to greet them. They happened to be standing right near the man I took to be the husband of the intercessor God had shown me. The woman herself was standing some 30 feet away, talking to someone else.

After conversing with my students, I met the man, who introduced himself as Eddie Smith, then a pastor on the staff of a Baptist church in Houston. Somewhat impishly, I decided I would test Eddie with a couple of rather tricky theological questions concerning intercession in order to see if this Southern Baptist knew much about it. Much to my surprise, he answered them perfectly!

Then I went over to his wife. She told me her name was Alice Smith. I immediately said, "You're an intercessor, aren't you?"

She raised her eyebrows and said, "How do you know?"

"God told me when I was up on the platform," I replied.

Alice looked jolted! Then she started crying! "I can't believe I'm talking to you!" she blurted. "Six months ago God told me to start praying for you and I have been praying for you constantly ever since. I never imagined I would actually meet you in person!"

Once she had calmed down, our conversation went on from there. Among other things, Alice told me what a blessing an article on intercession that I had written for a Vineyard magazine, *Equipping the Saints*, had been to her senior pastor. Doris and I then arranged to spend several hours with Alice and Eddie before we left South Korea. At one point I asked Doris, "Do you think Alice might be a candidate for a new prayer partner?"

"What are we waiting for?" Doris said. "We'd better invite her before we leave!"

As you know, this was a radical departure from our usual procedure. Alice had been a total stranger, and we had literally waited for months before inviting an internationally known intercessor such as Barbara Byerly to join our team. But we both had such a strong witness in our spirits that Alice was to be a partner that we asked her right on the spot! She immediately accepted, because she had already known for six months that God had assigned the job to her!

At that point Alice became an I-2 prayer partner. But a month or two later, as I was praying in my private prayer time, the word of the Lord came to me so strongly that for the first or maybe the second time that I could remember, I "journaled" the word. The whole thing was about my future direction and Alice Smith.

Among other things, God told me that Alice would be my most powerful intercessor for years to come. This seemed strange, because up to that time Cathy had been my most powerful intercessor. God did not clarify things at the moment, but only a few weeks later it became clear that He was giving Cathy another assignment. Meanwhile I had spoken to Alice about possibly switching from an I-2 to an I-1. I still marvel at the goodness of God in seamlessly providing us a new I-1 intercessor even before reassigning the one He had previously given to us.

Life-Saving Intercession

A couple of months after the transition, God seemed to seal this new relationship with a second incident in which I believe my physical life was again saved. Remember the first one, where Cathy prayed for me as I fell off the ladder? There were enough physical and tangible details connected with that to allow a reasonable case to be made for cause and effect. This second incident, however, can only be analyzed and interpreted spiritually, so the best I can claim is that my interpretation of the event leads me to the conclusion that Alice's intercession saved my life.

What happened?

Alice Smith, then 40, was a mother of four and a real estate agent. She was also a Bible teacher and conference speaker. She called me on November 23, 1990, to tell me what had happened to her on November 15. On that day, she had already been praying for Doris and me for two and a half hours when a change came over her and an incredibly intense spiritual battle began. In more than 16 years of engaging in high-level spiritual warfare, it was the most ferocious attack she had ever experienced. She logged "1:15 P.M." in her journal, and she knew that I was in grave physical danger.

As she continued to intercede, the Lord gave her a vision of a principality coming out of the south. Later information has led us to suspect that the source of this attack was the spirit of death, known as "San La Muerte," which we had been battling in Argentina throughout most of 1990. The story of that front-line warfare in Argentina is told in my book *Warfare Prayer*. Whether that spirit of death itself was directly involved or whether assignments had been passed through some sort of hierarchy of dark angels, we do not know.

Alice says, "The principality was as large as a man and it was hovering over Peter's left shoulder with an arrow in its hand pointing toward his heart. I was crying out, 'Save him, Lord! Have mercy and save him!' I asked the Holy Spirit if Peter was okay, and He replied, 'His life is in the balance!' Travail then poured out of me! I was under such labor of prayer that I crawled to the phone and asked Eddie to pray. Eddie later told me he thought I was dying, and he enlisted the senior pastor and some of the church intercessors to help. The battle became more intense. I cried for mercy, reminding the Father of His plans for Peter, speaking the Scripture, and warring against the forces of darkness. Then at 1:57 P.M., as quickly as it began, it suddenly ended! I saw a warring angel of the Lord come and snatch the arrow from the principality's hand, break it in two over his knee, and leave westward! The spirit of death just disappeared!"

Alice, as you can imagine, was totally fatigued by the time this battle ended. Her strength was gone. Her legs felt like spaghetti. She lay on the floor for a full hour and a half before she could get up and go about her business.

And me? All of this would have occurred between 11 A.M. and 12 noon in my time zone that day. Neither Doris nor I could recall any signs of danger around us at that time. However, we are persuaded that Alice successfully intercepted the spirit of death, much as a modern missile shield will destroy enemy missiles before they strike their target. The apostle Paul was thankful for Euodia and

Syntyche, who did spiritual warfare on his behalf. Doris and I are equally thankful for I-1 intercessors such as Alice who have taken many of the enemy's blows for us.

Intercessors Can Switch Roles

Because I am such a left-brained, analytical person, I find myself very comfortable with categories like I-1 and I-2. At the same time, I am aware that not all like to draw such lines. It is important to realize that even with the lines in place, God may push intercessors back and forth across them as He chooses, depending on the situation. Maybe the lines are not that important after all. Several of our I-2 intercessors have reported being called upon to do intense spiritual warfare as they prayed for us. And I am sure that such things have happened more than we realize, because veteran intercessors will only share such experiences when and if God specifically gives them permission to do so. Much happens through them that we will never know anything about.

As an example of this category crossing, a while ago one of our 1-2 intercessors was Cathryn Hoellwarth, then a member of our Sunday School class. One Sunday, I was away on a ministry trip and Cathryn was attending the evening service at the Anaheim Vineyard Fellowship, where John Wimber then pastored. It just so happened that Doris was sitting two rows in front of her. As Cathryn looked at Doris, suddenly she got a clear picture of my head surrounded by dark, oppressive clouds. She immediately began interceding for me, believing that I was in a life-and-death struggle!

Later in the week, Cathryn discovered that while she had been praying, I had been on a flight to Detroit and, for some unknown reason, I had blacked out on the plane. This had never happened before—and has never happened again since. The paramedics and ambulance were waiting for me in Detroit, but after a thorough examination they could find nothing wrong so they released me. I called Cathy Schaller the next day from Detroit and asked her if she had been praying for me. She said that she had felt no special urgency to pray for me at that time. Apparently God had chosen to call Cathryn to stand in the gap for that assignment. Cathryn later said, "I suppose God taps into the I-2 intercessors when the I-1 intercessors are not available at that moment." What a comforting thought! Who knows what the paramedics might have found if she had not prayed?

Workplace Intercessors

Most of what I have said about recruiting prayer partners assumes that the leader is a pastor with a congregation of believers or another kind of Christian ministry leader with a constituency of believers. Christian leaders in the workplace live and operate under a different set of circumstances, but they need intercessors just as much as their church counterparts do. Recruiting these prayer partners, however, presents a serious challenge.

Let me explain this by imagining a scenario. Suppose I connect with a Kingdom-minded leader in the Business Mountain (this would apply to the other mountains as well) who tells me that he is going through some difficulty. For years, his business had increased and increased each year—until two years ago, when it plateaued. He has tried everything he knows, but to no avail. What could be wrong? I might suggest that our enemy, Satan, could have perceived that my new friend was gaining excessive influence for the kingdom of God in the Business Mountain. Satan could then have built a spiritual stronghold over the business to curtail its influence. What can be done about that? In most cases, the businessman would not have the spiritual weapons or the experience in using them necessary to break the stronghold himself. He would need the help of intercessors who did have the spiritual gifts necessary to achieve such a victory.

Suppose the businessman agrees that, yes, he probably needs intercessors. His next logical question will be, "How do I get them?"

Up until a few years ago, that would have been a tough question for me to answer. I could have said, "Well, just pray about it and God will give them to you," knowing deep down that such a thing most likely would never happen. Or I could have said, "Ask your pastor." But suppose the person in question was a traditional Lutheran or Presbyterian. His pastor undoubtedly would know very little about the kind of intercession we are talking about here. He would probably say, "OK, I'll put you on the church prayer list." That's a nice thought, but it is not really the solution to breaking that stronghold.

Now I have a better answer: "Call Tommi Femrite!" Tommi, who has been one of my I-2 intercessors for a long time, received an assignment from God in 2008 to establish a for-profit company, Apostolic Intercessors Network (AIN), which provides professional-level intercession wherever needed. Tommi has recruited a team of more than 60 seasoned intercessors whom she monitors very strictly. One of her goals is to enable these intercessors to earn a full-time living using the gift that God has given them. Predictably, she has had to face criticisms from some in the religious community who object to those who "pray for pay." But she neutralizes these attacks very convincingly in her book *Invading the Seven Mountains with Intercession*.[3]

If my friend takes my advice and calls Tommi, she or one of her senior staff will schedule a day-long on-site evaluation. This visit will be paid for, just like a business compensates any other type of consultant they retain. At the end of the day, Tommi will meet with the owner and make her recommendations. In most cases, she will suggest more than one intercessor, because intercessors (like physicians in a hospital) have certain specialties. Here is how Tommi herself sums it up: "AIN rises to [the] challenge by coming alongside leaders to identify and develop intercessory prayer teams, which are custom-designed for their businesses."[4]

AIN now has clients in all seven mountains and has built a thick file of testimonies from those who have seen radical changes come to their fields of workplace ministry almost immediately after the professional-level intercession began. This is good because it helps

Christian leaders understand the new paradigm that AIN is pioneering. As Tommi says, "Often all it takes to change someone's mind regarding compensating intercessors is evidence of the fruit they bring. Business people have no problem paying someone, especially when that person produces."[5] She can count on one hand those clients who have been disappointed.

Filtering Out the Flakes

One of the most thought-provoking chapters in Cindy Jacobs's classic book *Possessing the Gates of the Enemy* is titled "Flaky Intercession." She describes flaky intercessors as "men and women who, for a variety of reasons, drift outside biblical guidelines in their zeal for prayer. They bring reproach on their ministries and confusion and division in the church."[6]

I have such a high regard for intercessors that I hate to think any of them could be less than angelic, but the reality is different, as we saw in the story of Pastor Paul Freedman earlier in this chapter. Fortunately, we are talking about a minority, and as books such as Cindy's circulate, the minority I hope will become smaller and smaller. While I don't have any solid research on the subject, my personal observations would lead me to believe that we have less of a problem with flaky intercession now than we did when Cindy first wrote her book some 20 years ago.

Nevertheless, intercessors can and do sometimes appear on the scene for wrong motives. I will mention six of those motives, which Doris and I have used as a checklist for attempting to filter out the flakes:

1. *Bragging rights.* Some intercessors derive great pleasure from bragging that "I am the one who prays for the pastor." The larger the church is, and the more inaccessible the pastor is to ordinary church members, the more acute is the temptation to do this bragging. The same will apply to any Christian leader in the church or in the workplace, especially those leaders who have more national and international visibility.

2. *A need for* control. This may be the most pernicious and pervasive characteristic of flaky intercessors. We saw it clearly in the woman who prayed for Paul Freedman and nearly caused disaster. Cindy Jacobs tells of "Estelle," whose prayer group "began to pray fervently that the pastor would 'see the light and get aligned with God'—which was synonymous with getting aligned with them." Estelle's mistake, Cindy says, was that "she felt that her 'revelations' were superior to what the pastor or elders heard from God."[7] Cindy then goes on to explain how this perverted tendency can be seen as an "Absalom spirit." Need for control is very dangerous and should not be tolerated in a prayer partner if it ever arises.

3. *Lust or* seduction. It is sad but true that some women, who may or may not be gifted intercessors, are tempted at times by the lusts of the flesh. Some of these are astute enough to recognize that the prayer partner relationship can be used as a potential pathway toward seduction. Most pastors have developed defense mechanisms against allowing this to happen in the counseling relationship, but some may be blindsided by trusted personal intercessors. One woman actually tried this strategy with me, but fortunately she was not very good at it! In fact Doris had discerned her intentions almost the moment she passed through her outer office into mine. This is not just a *little* flakiness; it is a *lot*!

4. *Sentimentalism.* "Praying for our pastor would be such a fine thing to do." "I would love to do this." "Our pastor is wonderful, and I could help him so much if he would only select me as a prayer partner." Statements like this reflect a low level of understanding of intercession in general, and wrong motives in particular.

5. *Pride.* Wrongly motivated intercessors are typically not able to handle the joy and spiritual stimulation that come from hearing from God and praying His will into being through the leader. Consequently they tend to think more highly of themselves than they ought. Almost all recognized intercessors have had battles with pride within themselves, and most are on guard against it constantly. Whenever pride raises its ugly head, they immediately

confess it and tear down the stronghold. Some seek help from other intercessors. But sadly some do fall prey to spiritual pride. It surfaces in many ways, one of the most destructive being a tendency to gossip about the pastor or about inside details of the ministry.

6. *Personal emotional needs*. The ministry of intercession seems to be a magnet for emotionally disturbed people. Experienced prayer leaders are well aware of this, and they have developed ways and means of handling such people without further compounding their emotional problems. But when troubled would-be intercessors go on to seek personal relationships as prayer partners, the dangers are obvious. Those who think, *If I could only be the pastor's personal* prayer *partner, I would be healed,* need to search for more viable forms of therapy.

I do not enjoy thinking about or writing about the potential deficiencies of intercessors, although of course it is important to do so. I much prefer to describe their positive characteristics, as I will attempt to do in the next chapter.

Reflection Questions

1. Discuss the story of Paul Freedman. How could his near-tragic mistake have been cut off at the roots?
2. How would you respond to a pastor's invitation for you to become an I-3 intercessor? How about an I-2? Why?
3. There is a difference of opinion as to whether I-2 intercessors should be recruited or whether the initiative should be left to God. What do you think?
4. Review and discuss the three parts of Cindy Jacobs's formula for recruiting intercessors.
5. Without mentioning names, see if you can give some concrete examples of individuals who may have acted on the wrong motives mentioned toward the end of the chapter.

A PROFILE OF PERSONAL INTERCESSORS

There was a time when I would not have been able to explain what a personal intercessor was. But now, after many years of experience with them, I have come to the conclusion that they are the elite in the kingdom of God. They are the Navy SEALs, the Phi Beta Kappas, the Olympic teams of God's community. In fact, soon after first forming my own team of personal prayer partners, I went through a season when I was both intimidated by the intercessors and envious of them.

I recall one particular morning when I was struggling with this matter before God in prayer. I said, "Father, please give me intimacy with You like I am seeing in these intercessors. I want to be like them."

Then came one of those moments that are few and far between for me (but which are daily bread for true intercessors), when I clearly heard God speaking to me in response to my petition. He first told me to take my pencil and draw three steps, which I promptly did.

God then clearly showed me that the intercessors were on the top step, and I was on the middle step. Multitudes would be found on the bottom step. He told me that He wanted me to be one of His middle-step persons—someone who was in close touch with the intercessors, but who also could help many people on the bottom move up the stairway. He said that a number of those whom I helped from the lower step to the middle step would then pass me and go on to the top step.

I sensed that I heard God say that my task was not to minister in the throne room, but to be outside the throne room helping others to come nearer. Meanwhile, those who were already in the throne room would be major players in bringing me closer and closer to God.

God also assured me that I did have clear access to Him. He affirmed what I knew about the priesthood of all believers. Access to Him was not in doubt; it was just a question of the degree of intimacy.

Furthermore, He showed me that His family is large and that He loves all His children. His perfect calling and desire for each child is for him or her to be in the place where he or she will be the greatest blessing to the greatest number of others. Not all of His children are as yet in the place He wants them to be, but He seemed to assure me that I was. He said that I was to rejoice in being where He wanted me to be rather than fret over where I was not.

I realize that I do not always hear God as clearly as I might, but I believe that was one of the times when I did. I was greatly relieved. Not that I wouldn't like to be an intercessor—I would. (Of course, I would also like to be a guitar player or an airplane pilot or a major league shortstop or a ventriloquist, just to name a few.) However, that is not who I am. Knowing that I am *not* an intercessor helps me relate to intercessors all the more creatively.

The Profile of Intercessors

I have come to know enough intercessors and to know them well enough to perceive an emerging profile. Not that every intercessor would score a "10" on each one of the items, but when the cumulative total is added up, they will score higher than most people.

Because of the nature of this book, the profile is naturally biased toward personal intercessors rather than general intercessors or crisis intercessors or warfare intercessors, but for the most part it will apply to all of the above.

They Have the Gift of Intercession

When God calls members of His family to a certain task or assignment, He provides them with the supernatural gifting to accomplish that task according to His will. For those He has called to the upper step or into the throne room as intercessors, He provides what I like to call the spiritual gift of intercession. I described this concept in some detail in chapter 2, indicating that those with the gift of intercession ordinarily pray from two to five hours a day. The only exceptions I have found are working mothers with young families or those who are engaged in a full-time ministry of their own. They would love to pray more than two hours a day, but they truly cannot carve the time out of their schedules. Even so, they rarely let a day go by without praying at least one hour.

I was comforted when I learned that I was not the first to suggest something we can regard as a legitimate spiritual gift of intercession. None other than the famous St. John Chrysostom of the fourth century discerned it also. In his commentary on Romans, Chrysostom mentions the gifts of prophecy, wisdom, healings, miracles and tongues, and then he says, "There was also a gift of prayer... and he who had this prayed for all the people." He adds that those who have this gift are known by much interceding to God, many mental groanings, falling before God, and "asking the things that were profitable for all."[1]

The two chief characteristics that I have observed in those with the gift of intercession are (1) that they love to pray, and (2) that they see more tangible results of their intercession than the average believer does.

Spiritual gifts most often come in the form of gift mixes. Certain pairings of gifts are quite common, such as pastor-teacher or deliverance-discernment of spirits. Many of those who have the gift of intercession also have the gift of prophecy. There is quite a broad overlap of the two gifts.

As we saw in chapter 2, those with the gift of intercession may have different ministries or assignments. The Bible says, "There are diversities of *gifts*, but the same Spirit. There are differences of *ministries*, but the same Lord. And there are diversities of *activities*, but it is the same God who works all in all" (1 Cor. 12:4-6, emphasis mine). This diversity surfaces very clearly in Tommi Femrite's Apostolic Intercessors Network (AIN), which provides professional-level intercessors, with their differing "ministries" or "activities," to Christian leaders in the seven mountains of society. Depending on the needs of the particular client, Tommi might assign list intercessors, crisis intercessors, issues intercessors, salvation intercessors, personal intercessors, financial intercessors, mercy intercessors, warfare intercessors, worship intercessors, government intercessors, people group intercessors, or prophetic intercessors.[2]

They Maintain a Close Relationship with God

I like the way my late friend Evelyn Christenson described her prayer time in an interview for *Christian Life* magazine. She said it was no longer a "grocery list" of a few minutes of praise and intercession as it once had been. "I've learned that my closet prayer time involves so much of His replenishing my emotional needs—with God and I exchanging our mutual love. There's much more listening on my part than before." Evelyn spoke for many fellow intercessors when she said, "My average day starts at 4:30 A.M. and I spend several hours alone with the Lord almost every day." Her absolute minimum, which she called "threadbare time," was two hours.[3]

All Christians have a desire to be close to God. However the honest truth is that for the majority of believers, the daily time set aside for prayer is relatively short, and the emotional feelings of closeness to God during those times are generally not of the level we've been hearing the intercessors describe. Intercessors are not average Christians any more than apostles or prophets or evangelists or pastors or teachers are. Part of intercessors' difference from others is not how many lost souls they lead to Christ, but their ongoing intimate relationship with the Father.

To give an example, relatively few believers would feel that their life goals were being fulfilled by spending 10 hours a day, 365 days per year, in prayer, as do the Sisters of Perpetual Adoration in Anchorage, Alaska. One of the sisters correctly says, "Many cannot understand our life style, not even many of our families." Then she goes on, "But for us, this has brought us very close to God, and fulfills our potential."[4]

Historically, one of the most famous intercessors was Julian of Norwich, who spent her life as an "anchoress," cloistering herself alone for prayer in the early fifteenth century. Her memory endures mainly because of her book, *Sixteen Revelations of Divine Love*, which profoundly describes her closeness to God. She directed her thoughts to those who "deliberately choose God in this life for love"—people she described as "the little and the simple." For a shortened version of her book, she chose the graphic title, *Comfortable Words for Christ's Lovers*.[5] The deep closeness of intercessors to the Father apparently has not changed much, at least over the past 600 years.

They Receive Words from God

An important part of what happens when intercessors spend long periods of time in very close relationship to God is that they frequently hear directly from Him. David Bryant, founder of the dynamic Concerts of Prayer movement, calls this the "strategy of silence." Implementing the strategy of silence involves going before

God to seek His direction even in what we should pray about and how we should pray.

Openness and obedience are keys to hearing from God. At times the instructions God gives are almost as unconventional as when He told Ezekiel to eat a scroll or to lie on his left side for 390 days or to shave his head and beard and burn one-third of his hair in the middle of the city (see Ezek. 3-5). But intercessors anointed for this strategy of silence have developed the discernment to know whether the instructions they receive are authentic or not.

Several years ago now, I was doing a church-planting seminar in Toronto. I called Cathy Schaller on Tuesday, and she prayed for me over the phone, which she customarily did. This time she sensed that God wanted to use me to "release gifts of healing." This message was hard for me to understand, because it had nothing to do with the subject of my seminar, nor was I in the habit, as some of my friends were, of praying to release new gifts in others. My understanding of spiritual gifts was a bit more conservative than that and Cathy knew it. She indicated that God would show me what to do the next day.

I expected that God would give me further instructions during my morning prayer time, but I got nothing. Meanwhile, Joseph Mak, one of our Fuller graduates, had called Doris a week previously, asking if I would pray for two sick people, one of whom was in the hospital, when I got to Toronto. I was reluctant because I ordinarily did not do that, but I sensed that God wanted me to do it this time, so I agreed. When I arrived in Toronto, Joseph told me that God had used his telephone call to Doris as the turning point in the sickness of Anisa, the woman in the hospital, and that she had been discharged. We then agreed to pray at the hotel on Wednesday afternoon.

Anisa was late for the appointment, but the other woman I was to pray for, Rita, was there with Joseph. Her finger had been injured in a badminton game, but when I asked her about it, she told me she was already healed. I asked how that had come about.

She replied, "I prayed and God healed me!" When I told her that this was very unusual, she said that it had happened to her many times. Then I asked her if she ever prayed for healing for others. She said, "No, I wouldn't dare. I have only told one other person about this other than you." By then I knew that she had the gift of healing, and I told her so. "No, not me," she protested. "I'm not a doctor like you!"

Before we left, Rita prayed for both Anisa and Joseph and saw God's healing power manifested in both of them. I then prayed that God would activate the gift of healing in Rita, and I exhorted her to begin using it, holding herself accountable to her pastor, Joseph Mak.

So far as I can recall, this was the first time I had ever ministered in this way, and it worked! Here is my point: The indication that this incident would be God's will came through a personal intercessor, Cathy Schaller, who was accustomed to practicing the "strategy of silence" and thereby discerning the will of God.

Who Is "Everett"?

During the period of time when our I-1 baton was being passed from Cathy Schaller to Alice Smith, Alice called me early one morning. I was in the midst of teaching a one-week Doctor of Ministry intensive course. She said that earlier that morning (Houston is two hours ahead of California), God had told her that there was a pastor named "Everett" in my class who was going through a difficult time in his life and to whom God wanted to minister.

When I got to class and inquired about "Everett," sure enough, Everett Briard, pastor of a Presbyterian Church in Canada, responded with total astonishment, almost unbelief, that such a thing could actually happen. We as a class prayed for him, and some of the other pastors ministered to him personally as well. He later testified to the class that he was feeling a definite change in his spiritual and mental outlook.

Nine months later, Everett wrote me a letter telling me how important Alice's word had become to him. "I had been struggling with many things for a long time," he confessed, "not the least of which was the inability to get rid of an underlying sense of meaninglessness, and periodic times of depression." He said that in a different seminar, two weeks after the word from Alice, he had heard a Christian psychologist say that only through therapy could a person be moved from low self-esteem and self-hate to high self-esteem.

But, Everett said, "God did that instantly for me during your class. He set me free and has given me a sense of newness in ministry. Things that used to throw me into deep despondency no longer have the power to do that. I am so grateful!"

You can imagine how grateful I was as well, seeing God use me as a relatively passive instrument to link a Houston intercessor with a Canadian pastor visiting in Pasadena, California, and to witness God's power manifested in a mighty way. Yes, intercessors do hear from God!

They Employ Prophetic Intercession

All intercessors hear from God on a regular basis, and most of them from time to time will move into prophetic intercession. For some, prophetic intercession is a core mode of almost all of their prayer ministry. Don Bloch, a workplace minister from Jacksonville, Florida, is an example of one who has an ongoing ministry of prophetic intercession. He prays on call from the Lord for situations all over the world.

Bloch says, "The Lord shows me events that are about to take place and asks me to pray for them. I believe God is calling many people to be intercessors and more and more He is giving the gift of prophetic intercession."[6]

Cindy Jacobs defines prophetic intercession as "an urging to pray given by the Holy Spirit for situations or circumstances about which you have very little knowledge in the natural. You pray for the prayer requests that are on the heart of God."[7]

Lois Main, an intercessor from Coalinga, California, could not sleep one night in April 1983. She sensed that she heard the Lord saying, "Pray for the people of Coalinga. Go out and pray now!"

Although it seemed to be a very strange time for such a general-ized assignment, Lois obeyed, got dressed, and faithfully walked the dark and deserted streets of Coalinga, praying for people in each building she passed. After a long period of time, she felt released to go back to bed and sleep the rest of the night.

Sure enough, the next afternoon Coalinga suffered a 6.5 earth-quake. The local hospital was braced and on high alert to treat all the trauma victims. Surprisingly, only 25 people showed up, most of them with only minor injuries.

Sondra Johnson, who tells this story, comments, "Intercessors must be willing to step out in faith and pray as God speaks to their hearts. Like most who pray prophetically, we might never know the results. But we must leave that to God, knowing we have done His will."[8] In this case, Lois Main had the added satisfaction of knowing the remarkable results!

They Are Quiet People

Although there are several notable exceptions to this rule, the great majority of authentic intercessors are quiet people. They do not particularly need or like to be up front. They do not care if their names are not widely known. In fact, some who have written books on intercession would prefer that their names be left off the book, although they somewhat reluctantly accede to the wisdom of ed-itors and publishers, who know that the book will be accepted as authentic only if it carries the name of the author.

Colleen Townsend Evans says that "aloneness" is one of the prices intercessors regularly pay. "As an intercessor," she says, "be prepared to spend some very quiet alone hours." Other people will not always know or understand what an intercessor is praying about. Evans says that intercessors "will be put in quiet corners where no one will know what we are doing, and God will seal our lips so that we are not to boast or talk about what we are doing."[9]

The apostle Paul might have had intercessors in mind when he said, "Those members of the body which seem to be weaker are necessary. And those members of the body which we think to be less honorable, on these we bestow greater honor" (1 Cor. 12:22-23). Although we may not see them much, the Body of Christ needs intercessors for a healthy life just as much as our physical body needs a pituitary gland, which we see even less.

They Prioritize the Leader

For personal intercessors—as opposed to other kinds of intercessors—the pastor or apostle or workplace leader or whoever they have been assigned to pray for is usually elevated to a high priority in the total prayer schedule. It does not happen every day, but it is not unusual for Doris and me to get reports that one of our intercessors has prayed for us for an hour or even several hours on a particular day. Keep in mind that we only hear about such situations when the prayer partner has been released by God to tell us, which I am sure is only a fraction of the times it actually occurs. Sometimes we learn exactly when they prayed; sometimes we never know.

One of the times of special intercession was on a Sunday evening when Cathy Schaller was ironing in her kitchen. At precisely 6:30, the Holy Spirit came on her for intercession, and she prayed for me until she was released at 7:00 P.M. She went back to her ironing and then called me the next morning to see why she had prayed.

Well, that Sunday evening, Doris and I had gone to Anaheim Vineyard, and before the service, we dropped in at Pastor John Wimber's office to have a Diet Coke with John and his wife, Carol. As we chatted, I told him of an event the preceding week where I had been privileged to pray for a six-year-old boy who had been born with no ears. Miraculously, the boy's ears started to grow out half an hour after the prayer session!

When John heard the story, he immediately asked me to share the testimony with the congregation that night. To say the least, I had not come prepared to speak to an audience of 3,000 people about an incident so dramatic that I myself had not had time to process it well. I knew that I needed to focus attention on the power of God, not on myself, and I needed to draw out an application for those in the congregation. I felt that I was in far over my head, but I obeyed John, took the microphone, and did what I could.

Surprisingly, the sharing went well. The congregation was visibly blessed. God was glorified! I give the credit for all of that to one of my personal intercessors, who heard from God and took a break from her ironing between 6:30 and 7:00, the exact time that I was on the platform at the Vineyard!

Because of priorities such as this, it is imperative that a potential intercessor be totally honest when considering a leader's request that he or she become an I-1 or I-2 prayer partner. There should be no sentimentality involved. And do not think that assigning such priorities implies exclusivity. I have mentioned that several of our prayer partners have been assigned to more than one leader at a time, and that the intensity of prayer for each one can and frequently does vary over time.

For example, the late Mary Lance Sisk, who was one of our long-term I-2 intercessors, also prayed for Leighton Ford and Joni Eareckson Tada. Other intercessors, however, do pray primarily for one leader at a time. Lil Walker is an example of that approach. Looking back, I am pleased that when I first invited Lil to become an I-2, she was honest enough to turn me down because she had been assigned to pray primarily for our pastor, Paul Cedar. Lil and I were good friends, so sentimentalism could have diverted her, but it didn't. Later, when God's timing was right, Lil became one of Doris's and my most dependable I-2 intercessors.

They Maintain Open Communication

A characteristic of most personal intercessors is that they maintain open communication channels with the pastor or other leader for whom they are praying. That is why it is best for both the leader and the intercessor to be aware of the prayer partner relationship. Secret prayer partners undoubtedly have some value, but some informal research done by intercessor Nancy Pfaff has confirmed the general consensus that their impact is limited.

Having an explicit prayer partner agreement opens the way to a covenant relationship in which each side can understand and agree upon mutual responsibilities. Some of the ingredients for such a relationship and some suggestions to keep the communication flowing well will come in the next chapter.

How long does the relationship last? It is usually for an indefinite time. As I have mentioned previously, I think it is best to assume from the start that it will be a long-term arrangement. Nothing is intrinsically wrong with recruiting a personal intercessor for, say, six months or a year, but in my opinion an open-ended agreement is preferable. Many intercessors feel that their assignment is for a lifetime, but circumstances may change on either or both sides, and God may direct that the relationship be changed.

They Protect Confidentiality

When Cindy Jacobs lists the qualifications of personal prayer partners, number two on her list (after a commitment to pray) is confidentiality.[10] Because Doris and I recruited our initial prayer partners from a group of people with whom we had already developed a trusted relationship over a long period of time, confidentiality did not at first occur to us as an important consideration.

I clearly recall, however, that when I first approached Barbara Byerly about the possibility of praying for us, she emphasized more than once that what we shared as prayer requests would be kept strictly confidential and that we could totally depend on it.

She said that she had known of cases where confidentiality had been violated and personal prayer requests had become subjects of gossip, doing much damage to leaders and their ministries. This was very important insight for us.

Fortunately, as the years have gone by, Doris and I have never been forced to go through any bad experiences in order to learn firsthand how important confidentiality is. From time to time, we do share items with I-1 and I-2 intercessors that are definitely not for public knowledge. In doing so, we have always felt that our shared information was as secure as the papers we keep in our safe deposit box. Only with this assurance can pastors and other leaders feel comfortable opening up their deepest and most urgent needs to the intercessors.

They Suffer Seasons of Dryness

It would be easy to put intercessors up on such a high spiritual pedestal that we forget they are human just like the rest of us. However, they themselves will be the first to remind us of their frailties. Intercessors have their ups and their downs. They have their good days and their bad days. They can leave a powerful mountaintop experience with God and from there plunge into the valley. One of our roles as leaders is to understand this and to nurture our intercessors through difficult periods just as they do with us.

A case in point: Some time ago, Alice Smith, when she was still our I-1 intercessor, made a memorable trip to Israel. After some intense and exhausting times of intercession and spiritual warfare, she felt that some significant battles had been won against high-ranking principalities. But the warfare took its toll. Soon after she returned, Alice wrote to Doris and me, saying, "I am in the midst of a very difficult time of dryness before the Lord. This is not uncommon to experience because intercessors have to have a spiritual 'tune up' every once in a while to see if they are praying for the benefits, or really praying and enjoying the Lord because of Who He is." Here again is the heart of an intercessor, who has no greater desire than a close relationship with God.

"Especially after a high spiritual experience such as I encountered in Israel," Alice went on, "there is often the tendency to press into the Lord for a 'bigger high,' while He is more interested in the quiet, still fellowship of knowing His presence." She seemed somewhat apologetic about the fact that when she prayed for us during this season, she was not hearing as much from the Lord as she usually did. She may have been apologetic to us, but she was not apologetic to the Lord, because she knew that He was monitoring her faithfulness at that point. She concluded her letter by saying, "These times always spark a fresh gratitude for when I do hear Him speak once again."

Soon afterward, as we all knew would happen, the dry period ended and things returned to normal. Meanwhile we had noticed that God was giving extra assignments to some I-2 intercessors. For example, it was during that time that Doris and I made the very significant visit to the March for Jesus office in London that I told about awhile ago. Alice Smith was not available at the moment, so God had Dave Rumph and Barbara Byerly step up to the plate and pray us through that whole historic experience.

They Need Help from Others

I have already mentioned the Aarons and Hurs whom God sends to support intercessors in times of need, just as He did for Moses. Often these supporting pray-ers receive spontaneous, one-time assignments. But some intercessors are taking pains to recruit ongoing teams of personal prayer partners of their own.

For example, Alice Smith maintains a very active prayer partners team, many of whom also have the gift of intercession. At one time, 13 of them committed to be I-3 intercessors for Doris and me. When Alice made that exhausting trip to Israel and then entered the subsequent "dry time," she assigned her own prayer partners to stand in the gap for us, which they did. During that time, Alice forwarded several notes they wrote to her, expressing what they thought they were hearing about us. A typical note would read, "The Lord has continued this past week to speak to me about Mr. Wagner. The following four words have come to me for whatever confirmation or invitation they might contain . . ."

Unfortunately, too many intercessors do not realize that they need prayer partners just as much as other leaders do. Years ago, when we were just beginning to learn about personal intercession and all that was involved in it, Christy Graham (who, as I have previously mentioned, is normally a crisis intercessor) unexpectedly received a longer-term assignment to be a personal intercessor for Cathy Schaller, who was at that time our I-1 intercessor. God told Christy that Cathy was absorbing many of the attacks of the enemy that would otherwise get through to me, and that Cathy herself needed more protection.

So Christy went to Cathy and told her that God had assigned her as a personal prayer partner. Cathy was so surprised that her initial reaction was, "Pray for *me*? Why do I need prayer? Is there something wrong with me?"

Christy wisely responded, "Well, is there something wrong with Peter? Why does he need prayer?" Cathy immediately saw the point and welcomed Christy as a prayer partner. I was fascinated that in this instance God never did assign Christy as a personal intercessor for me, but only for Cathy.

Evelyn Christenson, herself a seasoned intercessor, suggests that, when possible, intercessors pair off for mutual prayer support. She says, "Do you have someone who will pray for you and for whom you will pray?. . . Find one person with whom you can share the secret problems and needs of your life. Someone who cares and who will never, never divulge your secrets. Then fulfill the law of Christ by 'bearing one another's burdens' (see Gal. 6:2)."[11]

The Rewards

If I did not know better, I would be embarrassed at seeing the power of God flow so powerfully through my ministry, knowing full well that a major reason for this is the faithful intercession of my incredible prayer partners. I am the one who gets praised, the one who gets the honors, the one who gets paid for it. None of the above ordinarily comes to the intercessors. Nor do the intercessors even desire any of those rewards. One of the things my prayer partners are constantly praying for is that my ministry will bear great fruit in the lives of others; as that happens, I get the credit for it. And the intercessors are delighted that I do!

Remember Joshua and Moses? Joshua got the credit for being the general who defeated Amalek and won the battle of Rephidim. But the divine power to do that came through Moses' intercession. Moses was delighted that Joshua won the battle and received the accolades!

We need to understand, however, that intercessors do not go unrewarded for their ministry. For starters, I believe that their greatest reward awaits them in heaven. If believers in heaven form concentric circles around God's throne, the intercessors will undoubtedly be in the middle—right behind the 24 elders and 4 living creatures.

Meanwhile, in the here and now, intercessors also have their reward. They are thrilled to watch their prayers birth the purposes of God in the lives and ministries of pastors and other leaders for whom they are praying. Experienced intercessors see many things happening in their churches or in their sphere of the workplace. Most of those leaders will have no idea that their intercessors are fervently praying through certain issues. For the intercessors it can be a covert, not an overt, assignment. When their secret prayers are visibly—sometimes dramatically—answered, it is a true thrill and an ample reward for the intercessors.

Still, the consistent testimony I get from intercessors is that by far their greatest personal reward is their close relationship with the Father. More than most believers ever do, they experience the fullness of the love of God day in and day out.

How to Pray for Pastors

I own a number of prayer guides for leaders, all prepared by mature intercessors. As I examine them, I discover that these personal intercessors basically agree with one another about how to approach intercession. What are they saying? The guides presuppose three things: (1) that the intercessor has moved into the presence of God through worship and praise, (2) that they have a close personal communion with the Father, and (3) that their prayers are consistent with the Word of God. The manuals also state that their content should not be regarded as fixed formulas for prayer, but rather as outlines that should be used in conjunction with the flow of the Holy Spirit.

The guide I find most helpful was prepared by one of our I-2 intercessors, Elizabeth ("Beth") Alves, president of Intercessors International. It is found in the chapter of her book *Becoming a Prayer Warrior* called "Daily Prayers." For each day, Beth lists a topic with (1) subtopics, (2) Scripture passages, and (3) written prayers. According to the way God is leading at a particular moment, intercessors may use any or all three of the categories. Beth's desire is to provide a practical aid so that intercessors can be "obedient and faithful in 'standing in the gap' on behalf of missionaries, ministers, and spiritual leaders assigned for prayer."[12] Her general outline goes as follows:

- *Sunday:* Favor with God (spiritual revelation, anointing, holiness)
- *Monday:* Favor with others (congregations, ministry staff, unsaved)
- *Tuesday:* Increased vision (wisdom and enlightenment, motives, guidance)

- *Wednesday:* Spirit, Soul, Body (health, appearance, attitudes, spiritual and physical wholeness)
- *Thursday:* Protection (temptation, deception, enemies)
- *Friday:* Finances (priorities, blessings)
- *Saturday:* Family (general, spouse, children)

To conclude, I love the way Will Bruce puts it in his brochure, "Pastors Need Prayer, Too." He says, "No matter how well you pay your pastor, praise him or work for him, it is only through earnest, strategic prayer that you can ever really help him be an effective minister in the hands of almighty God."[13] Well said!

Reflection Questions

1. Do you know one or more persons whom you would regard as having the gift of intercession? Talk about them.
2. Look once again at the image of the three steps. Where would you locate yourself?
3. Do you believe that God really speaks as specifically as telling Alice Smith about Everett? Has something like this ever happened to you or someone you know?
4. What are some of the reasons intercessors need others to pray for them?
5. Using the daily prayer outline toward the end of the chapter, spend a few minutes praying for your pastor or for another leader by touching on all the categories mentioned.

MAINTAINING YOUR INTERCESSORS

I find it both comforting and encouraging to realize that we have ample evidence that leaders about whom we read in the New Testament depended on personal intercession for the power, strength and wisdom they needed to carry out their assignments.

Let's take the apostle Paul once again as an example. He requested personal intercession in a number of his letters, but nowhere in more detail than in his letter to the Ephesians. Why would that be? Perhaps it's because the church at Ephesus was born out of some of the most intense spiritual warfare of Paul's entire career.

In Ephesus, Paul had dealt with spiritual forces of darkness on every level—from evil spirits being cast out through handkerchiefs that were taken from him, to confronting the seven sons of Sceva, to burning magical paraphernalia, to Diana of the Ephesians being known by all as the territorial spirit over the whole region.

This is undoubtedly why, in his epistle to the Ephesians, Paul deals so much with topics such as spiritual warfare and the armor of God. New Testament scholar Clinton Arnold observes that in Ephesians there is "a substantially higher concentration of power terminology than in any other epistle attributed to Paul."[1] A weapon of spiritual warfare to which Paul gives a high profile is prayer. He says we are to be "praying always with all prayer and supplication in the Spirit" (Eph. 6:18). Powerful prayer is an essential component of intense spiritual warfare.

Intercession Protects Us

You will see that Paul brings up two specific lines of protection "against principalities, against powers, against the rulers of the darkness of this age, against spiritual hosts of wickedness in the heavenly places" (Eph. 6:12). The first is our individual protection, namely the whole armor of God (see Eph. 6:11-17). Each one of us has the responsibility of putting on the whole armor of God day by day. Pastors and other Christian leaders who fail to do this through either ignorance or indifference make themselves unnecessarily vulnerable to "the fiery darts of the wicked one" (Eph. 6:16).

The second line of protection against the enemy is intercession. In the Bible translation I use (*New King James Version*), the prayer passage beginning with Ephesians 6:18 is separated from the last verse of the whole armor of God passage (v. 17) by only a semicolon. Mentioning prayer is not simply a formality; it is an integral component of the actual weapons of spiritual warfare.

Paul requests, first of all, general intercession, which he calls "supplication for all the saints" (Eph. 6:18). Then he becomes much more personal and asks the Ephesian Christians to pray "for me" (Eph. 6:19).

Paul does not stop in this instance with a rather vague request for prayer—as he does, for example, when writing to the Thessalonians and saying simply, "Brethren, pray for us" (1 Thess. 5:25). No. He begs the Ephesians specifically to pray "that utterance may be given to me, that I may open my mouth boldly to make known the mystery of the gospel" (Eph. 6:19).

This is worth looking at, because here we see Paul, as the leader, requesting personal intercessors to focus their praying on effectiveness in his assigned ministry. As a cross-cultural church planter, his primary task was to make known the gospel, so he needed prayer especially for that task. Other leaders might be assigned different kinds of ministries according to their spiritual gifts. Think, for example, of Priscilla or Luke or John Mark or Titus or Philemon or others with whom Paul ministered. For the most part, they would have sets of spiritual gifts different from Paul's, so they would receive divine assignments different from his and consequently would need their personal intercessors to focus on whatever their ministries might be.

This brings us to the conclusion that to the degree that our intercessors pray for us, we gain protection from the fiery darts of the wicked one over and above the armor of God that we ourselves are responsible for using.

Leaders Do Receive Intercession

I would not want to give the impression that because personal intercession for leaders may be underutilized, it is not utilized at all. When I first researched this book, I wrote a letter to 35 celebrity leaders whose names were household words in the American evangelical community, and I was pleasantly surprised to find that 28 of them could name individuals who prayed for them on a regular basis. At least 19 of those would have been I-1 intercessors according to the definition I am using. This came out to be 54 percent—much higher than I might have guessed—possibly because of the select list of leaders to whom I wrote. I would like to think that this helps verify the point I am trying to get across. Could it be that one of the reasons God was able to entrust these individuals with positions of high visibility and influence was that they were actively depending on personal prayer partners?

A couple of interesting facts emerged from the survey. One was that the age of the intercessors seemed disproportionately high. A large number were in their sixties or above. Why might this be? Perhaps a combination of Christian maturity and retirement from vocational careers increases the eligibility and availability of many for serious intercession. There may be different reasons as well.

The other fact was that about one half of those who could name their intercessors named family members, such as spouses or parents or grandparents or grown children. I am not advocating that this pattern is ideal—I'm simply reporting.

Although James Dobson did not happen to be on my list, I learned a lot about him through his biography, *Dr. Dobson: Turning Hearts Toward Home*, in which author Rolf Zettersten reveals that Dobson depends greatly on personal prayer partners, two of whom he mentions. One is Dobson's wife, Shirley, who says that when they almost lost their children four times during a six-month period, she came under a great burden of prayer. Recognizing this as an attack of Satan, she says, "To counteract this, I bathed our children and Jim in prayer. I still spend one day a week fasting and praying for them."[2]

Dobson's other prayer partner was Nobel Hathaway, a widower and personal friend of Dobson's parents. Hathaway said, "I have committed my remaining days to continue the ministry of prayer that Dr. Dobson's parents started. I have a one-man prayer meeting for Jim, Shirley, Dana, and Ryan. I am committed to bombarding the skies with prayers for the Dobsons."[3]

Reinhard Bonnke, one of our generation's foremost crusade evangelists, has a ministry akin to that of the apostle Paul. Like Paul did, he depends heavily on intercession. At one point in time, Suzette Hattingh, with whom I had the privilege of working during the 1990s prayer movement, not only served as Bonnke's I-1 intercessor, but also mobilized massive prayer for each crusade. Before Bonnke preached, Suzette would have gathered literally thousands in a given city, instructing and releasing them for true intercession. Bonnke sees it this way: "It is not a case of singing choruses and praying for a blessing, but of pulling down the strongholds of Satan. Intercessors are a mighty battering ram."[4]

The Responsibility of the Leader

There may be exceptions, but intercession is not usually generated and sustained spontaneously. Pastors and other leaders must be open not only to receive intercession, but also to personally encourage their intercessors.

I was shocked to learn that some years ago, Reinhard Bonnke called in Suzette Hattingh and said, "At least five of the leading pastors of this nation have warned me not to form an intercession department in Christ for All Nations because of problems they told me they experienced with their personal and general intercessors!" I am glad to report that this did not deter Bonnke from establishing his ministry of intercession, but nevertheless he wisely took the precaution of asking Suzette to investigate.

Suzette then visited each personal intercessor of each of the concerned pastors. She found that they were frustrated, discouraged and disappointed because their pastors did not understand their responsibilities as leaders to their intercessors. The intercessors all agreed that there were four basic problems:

1. Lack of information
2. Lack of input and trust from the pastors
3. Lack of feedback on answered prayers
4. Lack of openness between leadership and intercessors

Since then, Suzette has had personal contact with thousands of serious intercessors. She says, "I have found the problems mentioned above among all levels of intercessors."[5]

Very frequently, when a ministry of personal intercession breaks down, the leader is at fault. When leaders are distant, indifferent and/or self-protective, many prayer partners will eventually lose heart and lay down their weapons—and both the leader and the intercessor fall short of what God wants them to be.

Maintaining the Intercessors

In the concluding paragraph of his letter to the Ephesians, Paul provides what I consider a practical model of how we as leaders should relate to our intercessors in order to maintain their interest and their faithfulness to do spiritual warfare on our behalf. By saying this, I do not mean to imply that our prayer partners' primary motivation is anything other than to serve God and obey Him. If God has called intercessors to pray for us, He will help maintain them. However, I also think that, in His providence, God entrusts us with a vital role in keeping the relationship alive and well.

Paul sensed this, I believe, when he told the Ephesians, right after he urged them to pray, that he was sending Tychicus to them. Back in those days—before postal service and telephones and faxes and email and cell phones—the preferred method of communication was by way of personal messenger. The messenger would often carry a written letter, as Tychicus undoubtedly did in this case, but the personal spoken words of the messenger were also vital.

What, then, was Tychicus supposed to do when he met the intercessors? Two things:

- Share personal information: "That you may know our affairs" (Eph. 6:22).
- Share Paul's love and encouragement: "That he may comfort your hearts" (Eph. 6:22).

Personal prayer partners typically do not make high demands of the pastor or other leader for whom they pray. But they are extremely grateful if we provide for them the information they need to pray intelligently, and if we, from time to time, encourage them with words of appreciation for their ministry on our behalf.

Pray for Your Intercessors

The relationship between leaders and intercessors should not be thought of as a symmetrical relationship. By this I mean that it is not like borrowing money that has to be repaid. For example, Joshua won the battle of Rephidim because he received Moses' intercession, even though, at least at the time, there is no indication that he returned substantial intercession back to Moses.

The term I have been using throughout this book, "prayer part-ners," has also been used by some to describe a reciprocal relation-ship, i.e., "You pray for me and I'll pray for you." This can be a very positive and fruitful arrangement. In the last chapter, for example, I mentioned how the late Evelyn Christenson recommended it. However, this is not the sense in which I have been using "prayer partners" in this book.

If I tried to repay the prayer I receive from my prayer partners, I would do little, day in and day out, other than pray. In my mind, attempting that would be about the same as attempting to repay Jesus for my redemption—impossible! So I have learned to receive their prayers thankfully as a gift of God's grace.

None of this means that we should fall into the trap of taking our prayer partners for granted. I follow a pattern of thanking God for each of my prayer partners by name every day. I keep a picture of each one pasted inside the front cover of my Bible, and from time to time I look at the pictures and pray for each one. I do not usually spend a long time on each one, but I do bring them all before God's throne. You may remember that Paul, in his letter to the Ephesians that we have been looking at regarding intercessors, says, "I . . . do not cease to give thanks for you, making mention of you in my prayers" (Eph. 1:15-16). This is what I make a habit of doing as well.

I should add that there are occasions when I do stop and pray at greater length for my prayer partners. For example, I often pray when I know that one of them is going through a particularly diffi-cult time. I also pray when they are part of a ministry activity with me. I remember that I prayed a good bit for Barbara Byerly and Mary Lance Sisk when they were gathering a team of intercessors to accompany us to Argentina in 1991 for our first annual Harvest Evangelism International Institute with Ed Silvoso. However, even during that period of time, they were praying much more for me than I was praying for them.

In fact, we all intensified our prayers for one another greatly after we suddenly discovered that a group of high-level Argentine

witches and warlocks had set up an "occult fair" in the same hotel we were using in Buenos Aires! They had arrived a week early
and were planning to block our attempts to spread the gospel of
the Kingdom. I never thanked God so much for our intercessors!
It was only because of them that the witches' chants, incantations,
hexes, curses and attempts at infiltration were totally neutralized.
Unbelievably, on the last day we were there, the government ex-
pelled the group from the hotel for illegally practicing divination!
A local newspaper ran a cartoon showing the witches flying out
of our hotel on broomsticks! Shades of Ephesus! We learned well
why Paul so greatly desired intercession!

Communicate Regularly

Communicating is the part that takes time. One of the best-known
cases in missionary history in which evangelism was stimulated
through prayer occurred when J. O. Fraser recruited prayer partners for his evangelistic work among the Lisu of Burma. For years
his preaching had produced virtually nothing. But this barren
season was teaching him something, namely that the real battle
for the Lisu was a spiritual one. He later said, "I know enough
about Satan to realize that he will have all his weapons ready for
determined opposition. He would be a missionary simpleton who
expected plain sailing in any work of God. I will not."[6]

Fraser wrote home to his mother, who for years had ministered
as what we would call his I-1 intercessor. He asked her to recruit
"a group of like-minded friends, whether few or many, whether
in one place or scattered" to join with her in prayer for the Lisu.
His mother immediately went to work—and the results were dramatic. The warfare obviously had been too great for just one intercessor. Once the group started praying, hundreds of Lisu families
began coming to Christ in a short period of time. However, while
that is notable in itself, it is not my primary point here. My point is
to indicate that when J. O. Fraser requested that his mother build

a prayer partners team, he was alert enough to add, "If you could form a small prayer circle, I would write regularly to the members."[7]

Fraser was very serious about this. He wisely said, "I am not asking you just to give 'help' in prayer as a sort of sideline, but I am trying to roll the main responsibility of this prayer warfare on you. I want you to take the burden of these people on your shoulders. I want you to wrestle with God for them." And his role? He saw himself as an intelligence officer. "I shall feel more and more that a big responsibility rests on me to keep you well informed."[8] He was prepared to invest the time necessary to communicate with his prayer partners.

I learned a great deal about this principle from John Maxwell while he was still pastoring Skyline Wesleyan Church in San Diego. He always gave communication with intercessors a high priority. The 100 men who prayed for him had privileges that other church members did not have, notably direct access to the senior pastor. John did not send a Tychicus to them, but instead he met with them personally four times a year—three times for breakfast and once on an all-day prayer partner retreat where they ate together, played together, learned together and prayed together. He met with one-fourth of them every Sunday morning before the service on a rotating basis. He would share his needs, and they would lay on hands and pray God's anointing on their leader. Once a month, John had lunch with his I-1 intercessor, Bill Klassen.

Doris and I try to write substantial letters to our I-1 and I-2 intercessors. We are very open and honest with them. When major decisions need to be made, they are the first to know, and they pray us through them.

Over the years, hardly anything has been more important than the decision we made in 1991 to coordinate the United Prayer Track of the AD2000 Movement under Luis Bush. Our prayer partners team had been organized by then, and they began to pray when we first started learning about the movement. After praying for many weeks, the intercessors began hearing—separately, not together—that the AD2000 Movement was indeed a major item on the heart of God for the 1990s, and that the invitation for us to be a part of it was clearly a call from Him. As much as anything else, these divine assurances through our prayer partners convinced us that God wanted us to make this high-level commitment, which turned out to have radical implications for our ministry career.

From Convergence to Afterglow

As you know, I wrote the first edition of this book more than 20 years ago. Rewriting it now has caused me to do a bit of introspection as I compare our current situation to that of two decades ago. As I look at this section about communicating with intercessors, I cannot help but notice some changes that have taken place through the years. Back then we wrote more frequently, we sent copies of some of my most vital correspondence, we sent certain reports that I had written or that we had received, we photocopied crucial articles, and we were highly intense. However, life seems calmer now and this, not surprisingly, is reflected in our give-and-take with I-1 and I-2 intercessors.

How can I analyze and explain these changes now that I am in my eighties?

To begin, I need to affirm that on this point I can only draw on personal experience. I cannot pretend that what has happened to us would necessarily be the right thing or the wrong thing for others in similar situations. Still, I'll try to be as objective as possible, with the hope that some may benefit from it.

J. Robert ("Bobby") Clinton was a colleague of mine on the Fuller Seminary faculty and a personal friend. His textbook, *The Making of a Leader*, has helped me a great deal in understanding how the different phases of leadership development ordinarily progress. When I first wrote *Prayer Shield*, I had entered what Clinton calls "Convergence." Convergence is the most productive phase of a leader's career. I entered Convergence around 1980 and it lasted some 30 years. When I look back at the 1980s and the 1990s and the 2000s, I have a hard time believing that I could sustain the energy necessary to accomplish what I did. I published my memoir, *Wrestling with Alligators, Prophets and Theologians*, in 2010, and sometimes I now get out of breath just reading parts of it. Whenever I do think back, I fully understand why Doris and I desperately needed a super, highly motivated, intense and well-informed intercession team, which, by the grace of God, we had firmly in place.

One area for which I especially needed prayer during Convergence had to do with my learning habits. I always seem to have been open to new ideas. As I mentioned earlier, when I recently took a long look at my 60 years of ministry, I was able to identify 17 significant paradigm shifts that I had experienced through the years. I tried to look at these as a reflection of Romans 12:2, where Paul tells us to be transformed by the renewing of our minds. So I decided to write a chapter on each paradigm shift, and Regal has now released the resulting book, *This Changes Everything*. My point here is that most of these paradigm shifts precipitated unsavory public controversy in which I was personally vilified by those who remained committed to the old paradigm. I have been called a fool and a deceiver and an animist and dangerous and a theocrat and a heretic and just about anything else one could imagine. It goes without saying that such attacks (which unfortunately could even border on word curses), especially at the hands of fellow believers, can open the doors for serious intrusions of Satan and the demonic world. I believe it was through my intercessors that God protected me from falling into the traps the enemy was setting.

Another area requiring much prayer involved my penchant for starting new organizations when the need for them would arise. I first depended on my prayer partners to help me decide which opportunities for starting new ministries I should embrace and which ones I ought to skip. Then, once I felt that God was assigning me to break some new ground, I would need intercession as I undertook the task. Each organization was designed to advance the kingdom of God and consequently would threaten the enemy and bring on many spiritual counterattacks. No wonder I sustained high levels of intense communication with the intercessors throughout these years of Convergence.

During my eightieth year—calendar year 2010—I moved from Convergence to Clinton's final phase of leadership development, Afterglow. Here is how he defines this stage: "For a very few, there is Phase VI, Afterglow. . . . The fruit of a lifetime of ministry and growth culminates in an era of recognition and indirect influence at broad levels. Leaders in Afterglow have built up a lifetime of contacts and continue to exert influence in these relationships. Others will seek them out because of their consistent track record in following God. Their storehouse of wisdom gathered over a lifetime of leadership will continue to bless and benefit many."[9]

I imagine that some leaders negotiate the transition from Convergence to Afterglow gradually; perhaps they are not even fully aware of what is happening. I, however, decided to make an abrupt shift. After observing a number of professional athletes finish poorly because they played too far past their prime, I thought it would be best for me to step out of my leadership roles while I still had most of my wits about me. When would this be? Why not at age 80? I was definitely slowing down physically, and I knew that my mind would follow suit in due time.

As 2010 approached, I was leading 12 organizations. By the end of the year, I had dissolved 2 of them, I had turned over 9 others to my spiritual sons and daughters, and I kept one, Eagles Vision Apostolic Team (EVAT), which existed only for me to serve other apostles who had desired to be aligned with me. I communicated thoroughly with my intercessors as this process unfolded. Doris and I think it was one of our lives' biggest and best decisions. Because the prayer partners were making crooked paths straight, we ended up winners. By now, every one of the 9 new leaders has made significant changes in the ministries I turned over to them, and every one of the changes has been for the better. They are doing amazing things I never could do nor ever even wanted to do! And Doris and I love Afterglow!

Most of our I-1 and I-2 intercessors saw us through the Convergence years, and they are all hanging in with us now for the long haul. We have never loved them more than we do now. I'm sure that many of them are continually fighting battles for us in the invisible world that we will know nothing about. One of our most pressing challenges in this season has involved the physical issues of old age, especially Doris's surgeries on arthritic joints. At one point we were letting down on communicating Doris's condition to the intercessors. Some of them complained, so we approached Becca Greenwood, one of our I-2s who lives near us, to become what we are now calling an "I-1.5" prayer coordinator. I am still traveling nationally and internationally approximately 140 days a year, so the intercessors have my itinerary and pray me through the various assignments. There is and will continue to be plenty for which we need prayer in Afterglow, but compared to Convergence the total burden is much lighter.

Avoid the Dangers

One of the celebrities whom I contacted regarding their personal intercessors replied with a serious letter expressing a degree of anxiety that he felt over the whole idea. This blindsided me because I imagined that every leader would want intercessors. Fortunately, not too long after receiving the letter, I mentioned it to my friend Pastor Casey Treat of Christian Faith Center in Seattle, who explained some background that helped clear things up.

It seems that in the early 1980s, a wave of fanaticism rose up concerning intercession, particularly among the "word of faith" stream, but also among other charismatics. Some pastors began to ride hobby horses (going to extremes or on tangents) and taught that if you did not pray three to five hours per day, you could not possibly be moving in the Spirit. They picked up on Paul's "travail" or "laboring in birth" analogy from Galatians 4:19. Some intercessors then began to groan loudly as if in labor and even lie on top of one another on the church platform! Unfortunately, this display of flaky intercession, as well as other similar behaviors, was prevalent for some time. Some flaky fasting was also involved, based on the questionable premise that the longer you fast, the more you can get God to do what you want Him to do.

The good news is that this was only a fad and we see little of it today. The bad news is that memories of it are still strong enough for some pastors to be very cautious about personal intercession. Casey Treat himself has a fine team of prayer partners. He introduced me personally to his three I-1 intercessors, each of whom has a particular specialization for their prayer ministry.

Even where the intercession itself may not be flaky, dangers inherent in receiving intercession need to be recognized and avoided. I have been stressing that intercession for pastors and other Christian leaders is a high-level spiritual activity. As such it can be expected to attract the attention of the devil in a high-level way. He will attack the relationships between a pastor and his or her intercessors in any way possible, but he seems to focus on three principal areas: spiritual dependency, emotional dependency and physical dependency. Let's look at these risks one at a time.

Spiritual Dependency

It is a dangerous mistake for the pastor or leader to become spiritually dependent on the intercessors. If this happens, the intercessors can become a substitute for the pastor's own personal interaction with the Lord. Judson Cornwall says that as he travelled across America, "Often I found pastors dependent completely on the prayers of a few old-timers, known as 'intercessors,' for the pastors themselves had virtually no private prayer ministry. This may well explain the staleness, the decline in morality, and the great insecurity that seems to characterize much of America's clergy."[10]

If you as a pastor or other leader feel that you might be falling into the trap of cutting back on your personal prayer life, I suggest that you do something about it with no hesitation. In chapters 4 and 5, I strongly stressed the need for us as leaders to develop quality prayer lives of our own, precisely so that we could avoid spiritual dependency. If it has been some time since you read them, I suggest that you review those chapters.

Also start reading some good books on prayer, such as Dutch Sheets's *Intercessory Prayer*, Dick Eastman's *The Hour that Changes the World*, Cindy Jacobs's *The Power of Persistent Prayer*, James Goll's *Prayer Storm*, Eddie and Alice Smith's *The Advocates*, Larry Lea's *Could You Not Tarry One Hour?*, Bill Hybels's *Too Busy Not to Pray*, or my book *Praying with Power*. You will undoubtedly have other books on the subject in your library.

It is one thing to wake up on the occasional morning and say, "Lord, I'm wiped out! Please let the intercessors carry the day." It is quite another to make a habit of doing this. No quantity or quality of intercessors can substitute for the pastor or other leader being an authentic man or woman of God.

Emotional Dependency

Cindy Jacobs warns, "The partners might become emotionally wrapped up in you, or you in them, in a way that is not healthy."[11] This does not mean that you could not have an especially close relationship with one or more intercessors, but it does mean that the relationship must at all times be an objective one.

If you find yourself emotionally down when the intercessor is down, take it as a danger sign. The intercessor (unless he or she is a spouse or other close family member) should never become a focal point of personal fulfillment. To think, *If I lost my intercessor, I wouldn't be able to go on with my ministry*, is likely a sign of emotional dependency.

Some have used the term "emotional adultery." Physical adultery means delivering your body to another; emotional adultery is delivering your soul. There is a clear line between friendship and affection. Crossing that line with an intercessor is forbidden and can lead to disaster. The leader can become so dependent that he or she feels that all important decisions need to be cleared through the intercessor, inadvertently inviting the intercessor to take control. No healthy intercessor wants that kind of control, which among intercessors could even be termed a "dirty word" and taken as an insult!

Physical Dependency

I think I have already said enough about immorality in the ministry to leave no doubt that this has become one of Satan's most effective tools in crippling the Church in our day and age. It should come as no surprise to us to suggest that Satan would like to destroy relationships between pastors and intercessors through inappropriate physical contact.

Psychological research has shown that most cases of pastoral indiscretion have been sparked in the counseling relationship; contacts with staff members take second place. I am happy to report that so far I have not heard of immoral physical relationships between pastors and their intercessors, although I do know of one pastor's long-time I-1 intercessor running off with the pastor's father!

To be sure, inappropriate contact is a constant danger that needs to be understood and avoided. Research shows that the majority of pastors are male and the majority of intercessors are female. This situation is not likely to change anytime in the near future.

To avoid any possibility of wrong contacts, some pastors, such as John Maxwell, relate only to prayer partners of their own gender. This does not mean that either John or his wife, Margaret, has any kind of excessive phobia about John's relating to women in the general course of his pastoral ministry. He relates as appropriately as any.

I was curious enough about this to interview John specifically concerning this danger when he was pastor at Skyline Wesleyan. He responded that his general policy is always to play to his strengths, and he is especially equipped to lead men. His gifts are such that men enjoy following his leadership. Not only was he receiving prayer from the 100 men who were his intercessors, but he also discipled them in their Christian faith. He called his prayer partners his "farm team" for the church board. No one was nominated to the board who had not been a prayer partner. Maxwell does not teach that all pastors should have the same policy he followed, but it goes without saying that those who are vulnerable to certain temptations would do well to follow his example. Either that or they should recruit family members as prayer partners.

For others, having female intercessors for male leaders works well. I have mentioned that I believe two of Paul's intercessors were Euodia and Syntyche, both women. I strongly suspect that, as I also brought up earlier, Mary, the mother of John Mark, could have been Peter's I-1 intercessor. And, of course, two of my own I-1 intercessors have been female.

To cause physical dependency, the enemy uses lust, inappropriate language and inappropriate contact. In order to avoid any of this, common sense is required. For a starter, the pastor or other leader must have a solid marriage as a prerequisite to relating to an I-1 intercessor of the opposite sex. There needs to be an open relationship between the spouses as well. The danger of physical indiscretion should be mutually recognized and assiduously avoided. Cindy Jacobs recommends, "Do not meet with a member of the opposite sex for prayer without someone else present."[12] I would go so far as to say that the less one-on-one contact there is between a leader and a member of the opposite sex the better.

In summary, I would like to suggest that both the leader and the intercessor should recognize these three principles. The role of the intercessor is:

- A close personal relationship, but not excessive intimacy.
- A strong influence in the life of the leader, but not manipulation or control.
- Partnership in ministry, but not ownership of ministry.

Go and Do It!

Steven Johnson, president of Word Indigenous Missions, once took a missions course with me at Fuller Seminary. Several months later, he wrote me a letter, reminding me that I had mentioned personal intercession rather briefly in one of the classes. I had simply encouraged those who did not have intercessors to go and do it.

He said, "As president of a world-wide church planting ministry I had found myself under severe spiritual attack. This resulted in extreme fatigue, the vexing of my soul, as well as spiritual attacks on my family." So Steve did it—he formed a team of prayer partners for the first time.

"Results of this were overwhelming," Steve reports. "Within days of sending the letter, I sensed a tremendous lifting of spiritual oppressions. I sensed a freedom concerning a warfare that was attacking my family as well as my personal ministry." He attributes all of this to the power released by God through his new prayer team. "In these last ten months," he says, "I can give testimony to being significantly different than in the months and years prior to having this prayer team."

Why not be like Steve Johnson? Go and do it!

Reflection Questions

1. What can we learn from the apostle Paul's attitudes toward his personal intercessors?
2. See if you can think of and name any leaders who are, in fact, receiving personal intercession. If you can't think of any, discuss why personal intercession may not be recognized and utilized as much as it could be.
3. Why is it that the leader needs to pray for the intercessors, but not as much as the intercessors pray for the leaders?
4. Discuss how the three danger areas of spiritual, emotional and physical dependency impact Christian leaders.

5. Talk about plans you might have to implement some of the things you learned from this whole book.

ENDNOTES

Introduction to the Second Edition

1. Charles G. Finney, *Lectures on Revivals of Religion* (New York: Leavitt, Lord & Company, 1835), p. 219.
2. Ibid., p. 218.
3. Ibid.
4. E. M. Bounds, *The Complete Works of E. M. Bounds on Prayer* (Grand Rapids, MI: Baker Book House, 1990), p. 486.
5. Cindy Jacobs, *Possessing the Gates of the Enemy* (Grand Rapids, MI: Chosen Books, 2009).
6. If the notion of apostles and apostolic ministry is new to you, you can familiarize yourself with the topic by reading my book *Apostles Today* (Ventura, CA: Regal Books, 2006).
7. The best analysis of this seismic shift is Ed Silvoso's book *Transformation* (Ventura, CA: Regal Books, 2007).
8. For further insight on this subject, see my book *The Church in the Workplace* (Ventura, CA: Regal Books, 2006).
9. An excellent introduction to the "Seven Mountains" is Robert Henderson's book *A Voice of Reformation: An Apostolic and Prophetic View of Each of the Seven Mountains in a Reformed State* (Colorado Springs, CO: Robert Henderson Ministries, 2010).
10. Tommi Femrite, *Invading the Seven Mountains with Intercession* (Lake Mary, FL: Creation House, 2011).
11. Elmer Towns, *Walking with Giants* (Ventura, CA: Regal Books, 2012), p. 227.
12. Ibid.

Chapter 1: The Power of Personal Prayer Partners

1. Walter Wink, "Prayer and the Powers," *Sojourners*, October 1990, p. 10.
2. Larry Lea, *Could You Not Tarry One Hour?* (Altamonte Springs, FL: Creation House, 1987), pp. 43-46.
3. P. J. Mahoney, "Intercession," *The New Catholic Encyclopedia* (New York: McGraw-Hill Book Company, 1967), p. 566.
4. See Alice Smith, *Beyond the Veil: God's Call to Intimate Intercession* (Houston, TX: SpiritTruth Publishing Co., 1996).
5. Dutch Sheets, *Intercessory Prayer* (Ventura, CA: Regal Books, 1996), p. 29.
6. Public domain.
7. John Calvin, *Institutes of the Christian Religion* (Philadelphia: The Westminster Press, 1960), p. 851.
8. Ibid., p. 853.
9. Jack W. Hayford, *Prayer Is Invading the Impossible* (Alachua, FL: Bridge-Logos, 2002), p. 93.
10. Walter Wink, *Unmasking the Powers* (Philadelphia, PA: Fortress Press, 1986), p. 91.
11. Dutch Sheets, *The Beginner's Guide to Intercession* (Ventura, CA: Regal Books, 2001), p. 18.
12. For more information on this crucial question of "open theism," see my chapter, "From Classical Theism to Open Theism," in *This Changes Everything* (Ventura, CA: Regal Books, 2013), pp. 137-148.
13. Some may be interested to know that a scholarly, exegetical study of these Pauline requests for personal intercession may be found in Gordon P. Wiles, *Paul's Intercessory Prayers* (Cambridge, England: Cambridge University Press, 1974), pp. 259-296.

14. Ralph P. Martin, *The Epistle of Paul to the Philippians* (Grand Rapids, MI: Wm. B. Eerdmans Publishing Co., 1959), p. 168.
15. F. F. Bruce, *The Pauline Circle* (Grand Rapids, MI: Wm. B. Eerdmans Publishing Co., 1985), p. 85.
16. D. Edmond Hiebert, *Personalities Around Paul* (Chicago, IL: Moody Press, 1973), p. 166.
17. F. W. Beare, *A Commentary on the Epistle to the Philippians* (London: Adam & Charles Black, 1959), p. 145.
18. Edwin B. Stube, *According to the Pattern* (Baltimore, MD: Holy Way, 1982), p. 84.

Chapter 2: The Intercessors
1. Robert Andrescik, "An Audience of One: An Interview with Ron Kenoly," *Ministry Today* (March/April 2004), p. 17.
2. Tim Hughes, *Here I Am to Worship* (Ventura, CA: Regal Books, 2004), pp. 62-63.
3. C. Peter Wagner, *Your Spiritual Gifts Can Help Your Church Grow* (Ventura, CA: Regal Books, 2005), p. 74.
4. Ibid., p. 70.
5. Copyright 1989 by WORD Music (a Div. of WORD, Inc.). All rights reserved. Used by permission.
6. See Tommi Femrite, *Invading the Seven Mountains with Intercession* (Lake Mary, FL: Creation House, 2011), pp. 170-184. Tommi adds: Issues Intercessors, Salvation Intercessors, Financial Intercessors, Mercy Intercessors, Worship Intercessors, Government Intercessors, People Group Intercessors and Prophetic Intercessors.
7. Ibid., p. 170.
8. Christy Graham, "The Ministry of Intercession," *Body Life,* Newsletter of 120 Fellowship Sunday School Class (Pasadena, CA, July 1987), p. 7.
9. For more information on strategic-level intercession, I recommend Cindy Jacobs's *Possessing the Gates of the Enemy*, Rebecca Greenwood's *Authority to Tread*, and my book *Warfare Prayer*.
10. Cindy Jacobs, *Possessing the Gates of the Enemy* (Grand Rapids, MI: Chosen Books, 2009), p. 66.
11. Graham Fitzpatrick, *How to Recognize God's Voice* (Chichester, England: Sovereign World, 1989), p. 48.

Chapter 3: Why Pastors Need Intercession
1. "How Common Is Pastoral Indiscretion?" *Leadership Journal,* Winter 1988, pp. 12-13.
2. Nancy Pfaff, "Christian Leadership Attributes Dynamic Increase in Effectiveness to the Work of Intercessors," *Journal of the North American Society for Church Growth*, 1990, p. 82.
3. Ibid., p. 83.

Chapter 4: Secrets of Pastors' Prayer Lives
1. Mark K. Littleton, "Some Quiet Confessions About Quiet Time," *Leadership Journal,* Fall 1983, p. 81.
2. Terry C. Muck, "Ten Questions About the Devotional Life," *Leadership Journal,* Winter 1982, p. 37.
3. "'Nones' on the Rise," PewResearch: Religion & Public Life Project, October 9, 2012. http://www.pewforum.org/2012/10/09/nones-on-the-rise/ (accessed January 2012).
4. Littleton, "Some Quiet Confessions," p. 81.
5. Ibid.
6. Richard J. Foster, *Celebration of Discipline (*San Francisco, CA: Harper & Row Publishers, 1988), p. 35.
7. Littleton, "Some Quiet Confessions," p. 82.
8. Muck, "Ten Questions," p. 34.

9. C. Kirk Hadaway, *Church Growth Principles: Separating Fact from Fiction* (Nashville, TN: Broadman Press, 1991), p. 164.
10. Thom S. Rainer, *Effective Evangelistic Churches* (Nashville, TN: Broadman & Holman Publishers, 1996), p. 67.
11. Ibid., p. 71.
12. "Status of Global Mission, 2013, in the Context of AD 1800-2015," *International Bulletin of Missionary Research*, vol. 37, no. 1, January 2013, p. 33.

Chapter 5: Receiving Personal Intercession
1. Charles Henry Robinson, *The Conversion of Europe* (London, England: Longmans, Green and Co., 1917), p. 378.
2. Colin Whittaker, *Seven Guides to Effective Prayer* (Minneapolis, MN: Bethany House Publishers, 1987), p. 111.
3. Richard J. Foster, "The PTL Scandal," *Charisma & Christian Life*, March 1988, pp. 39-44.
4. Gordon MacDonald, *Rebuilding Your Broken World* (Nashville, TN: Thomas Nelson, 2003), p. 213.
5. J. Lee Grady, "7 Ways to Stop the Adultery Epidemic," *Charisma Magazine*, May 8, 2013. http://charismamag.com/blogs/fire-in-my-bones/17642-7-ways-to-prevent-a-moral-failure? (accessed January 2014).
6. Jimmy Swaggart, "From Me to You," *The Evangelist*, April 1987, p. 58.
7. E. M. Bounds, *E. M. Bounds on Prayer* (Peabody, MA: Hendrickson Publishers, 2006), p. 137.
8. Jimmy Swaggart, "The Lord of Breaking Through," *The Evangelist*, March 1988, p. 7.
9. "Swaggart's Confession," *Charisma & Christian Life*, April 1988, p. 20.
10. Ibid.
11. Mark L. Bubeck, *Overcoming the Adversary* (Chicago, IL: Moody Press, 1984), pp. 44-46.
12. Ibid., p. 45.

Chapter 6: Three Types of Personal Intercessors
1. E. M. Bounds, *Purpose in Prayer* (Ada, MI: Flemming H. Revell Company, 1920), p. 149.
2. Ibid., p. 150.
3. Ibid.
4. From personal correspondence.
5. Thom S. Rainer, *Effective Evangelistic Churches* (Nashville, TN: Broadman & Holman Publishers, 1996), p. 66.
6. Pam Marhad, "Using Our Gifts to God's Glory," *Body Life*, Newsletter of 120 Fellowship Sunday School Class (Pasadena, CA, February 1990), p. 7.
7. Sylvia R. Evans, "Watching in Prayer," *Intercessors for America Newsletter*, June 1989, p. 2.

Chapter 7: Recruiting Prayer Partners
1. Cindy Jacobs, *Possessing the Gates of the Enemy* (Grand Rapids, MI: Chosen Books, 2009), p. 155.
2. Ibid., p. 151.
3. "The seven mountains" that we find in Femrite's title are a template that is being used widely for designing Kingdom strategies aimed at transforming society. The mountains, or spheres of society, are: religion, family, education, media, government, arts and entertainment, and business. One of the several good books on the subject is Robert Henderson's *A Voice of Reformation*.
4. Tommi Femrite, *Invading the Seven Mountains with Intercession* (Lake Mary, FL: Creation House, 2011), p. 204.

5. Ibid., p. 207.
6. Jacobs, *Possessing the Gates of the Enemy*, p. 120.
7. Ibid., pp. 120-121.

Chapter 8: A Profile of Personal Intercessors

1. Philip Schaff, ed., *A Select Library of the Nicene and Post Nicene Fathers of the Christian Church*, *Vol. XI: Saint* Chrysostom (Grand Rapids, MI: Wm. B. Eerdmans Publishing Company, 1956), p. 447.
2. You can find explanations of each of these ministries of intercession in Tommi Femrite's book, *Invading the Seven Mountains with Intercession* on pages 169-184.
3. Judith Couchman, "The High Cost of Prayer: An Interview with Evelyn Christenson," *Christian Life*, January 1987, p. 12.
4. Charles Hillinger, "Isolated in Anchorage Cloister, Nuns Say They Feel Closer to God," *Los Angeles Times*, December 23, 1989, p. 84.
5. J. Walsh, "Julian of Norwich," *New Catholic Encyclopedia*, Vol. VIII (New York: McGraw-Hill Book Company, 1967), pp. 48-49.
6. Barbara White, "Called to Prophetic Intercession," *The Breakthrough Intercessor*, January-February 1991, p. 5.
7. Cindy Jacobs, *Possessing the Gates of the Enemy* (Grand Rapids, MI: Chosen Books, 2009), p. 138.
8. Sondra Johnson, "Obeying the Call," *The Breakthrough Intercessor*, January-February 1991, p. 4.
9. Colleen Townsend Evans, "The Cost of Intercession," *The Breakthrough Intercessor*, January-February 1991, p. 1.
10. Jacobs, *Possessing the Gates of the Enemy*, p. 156.
11. Evelyn Christenson, *What Happens When Women Pray* (Wheaton, IL: Victor Books, 1975), p. 100.
12. Elizabeth Alves, *Becoming a Prayer Warrior* (Ventura, CA: Regal Books, 1998), pp. 167-210.
13. Will Bruce, "Pastors Need Prayer, Too" (Robesonia, PA: Overseas Missionary Fellowship).

Chapter 9: Maintaining Your Intercessors

1. Clinton E. Arnold, Ephesians: *Power and Magic* (Cambridge, England: Cambridge University Press, 1989), p. 1.
2. Rolf Zettersten, *Dr.* Dobson: *Tuning Hearts Toward Home* (Dallas, TX: WORD INC., 1989), p. 65.
3. Ibid., p. 169.
4. Reinhard Bonnke, *Evangelism by Fire* (Eastbourne, England: Kingsway Publications, 1989), p. 217.
5. Personal correspondence from Suzette Hattingh (March 23, 1992).
6. Eileen Crossman, *Mountain Rain* (Robesonia, PA: OMF Books, 1982), p. 65.
7. Ibid., p. 64.
8. J. O. Fraser, *The Prayer of Faith* (Robesonia, PA: OMF Books, 1958), p. 12.
9. J. Robert Clinton, *The Making of a Leader* (Colorado Springs, CO: NavPress, 2012), p. 40.
10. Judson Cornwall, *The Secret of Personal Prayer* (Altamonte Springs, FL: Creation House, 1988), pp. 9-10.
11. Cindy Jacobs, *Possessing the Gates of the Enemy* (Grand Rapids, MI: Chosen Books, 2009), p. 157.
12. Ibid., p. 158.

Index

Made in the USA
Columbia, SC
10 October 2020